Resocialization Series

Sheldon R. Roen, Ph.D., Editor

Reference Group Theory
and Delinquency

REFERENCE GROUP THEORY
AND DELINQUENCY

By
ROBERT E. CLARK

Behavioral Publications   **New York**
1972

Library of Congress Catalog Card Number 72-5755
Standard Book Number 87705-031-7-Cloth
87705-090-2-Paper

BEHAVIORAL PUBLICATIONS, 2852 Broadway—
Morningside Heights, New York, New York 10025

Printed in the United States of America

Library of Congress Cataloging in Publication Data

Clark, Robert E   1912-
    Reference group theory and delinquency.

    (Resocialization series)
    Bibliography: p.
    1. Reference groups. I. Title. [DNLM: 1. Group
Processes. 2. Juvenile Delinquency. 3. Social Be-
havior. HM 131 C594r 1972]
HM131.C739   301.18   72-5755
ISBN 0-87705-031-7

Contents

1. INTRODUCTION

In this book it is contended that the generally accepted differential association theory of Edwin H. Sutherland is a special case of the broader theory of reference groups as found in the writings of such authors as Herbert Hyman, Theodore Newcomb, Ralph H. Turner, and Muzafer and Carolyn Sherif.

Although it is difficult to determine the source of all of one's ideas, it is helpful in understanding a man to know something about the origin of some of his ideas. Edwin H. Sutherland (1942, p. 16) has helped us to understand his conception of the differential association theory by attributing to Louis Wirth some very germinal ideas. In an article by Louis Wirth (1931) two complementary views of delinquency were presented, the individual and the cultural. It was the latter view which influenced Sutherland the most.

Louis Wirth, drawing upon the psychiatric approach of William Healy, who had considered delinquency as the result of mental conflict within the individual, suggested in his 1931 article that a parallel to the inner conflict was to be found in the form of culture conflict. He presented ample evidence that crime was related to the conflict of cultures on a community basis. Low crime rates were found in small isolated communities which had homogeneous cultures and few status differentials. High crime rates were evident in heterogeneous communities,

1

particularly urban areas where the foreign-born population produced children who were subject to the cultural demands of their parents' Old World culture on the one hand and their foreign and American playmates on the other hand. These second generation immigrants quickly established primary social contacts with neighborhood play groups, many of which were delinquent gangs, and assimilated their culture. Included in the culture conflict theory of crime was recognition of the fact that each community had a different set of conflicting cultural influences, and mutually antagonistic groups. Each gang and each family had a culture of its own, competing with the others for the allegiance of individuals. In delinquent areas the influence of the gang exceeded the influence of the family and other conventional groups, requiring and demanding that its members follow its norms and take on its attitudes toward law and order.

The individual side of culture conflict, also described by Louis Wirth (1931, p. 490), is found in the following statements:

"The sociological study of delinquency ... does not end with a general description nor even a careful analysis of the cultural milieu of the individual. On the contrary, the study of the culture on the objective side must be complemented through a study of the personal meanings, which the cultural values have for the individual....

"If the conduct of the individual ... is seen as a constellation of a number of roles either integrated or mutually conflicting, each of which is oriented with reference to a social group in which he has some sort of place, we can appreciate the significance of understanding these cultures for the control of the conduct of the individual. But the important features of each cultural situation are not immediately evident to the observer and do not constitute objectively determinable data. They must be seen in terms of the sub-

jective attitudes of the individual, which, as
our experience shows, can best be determined
by means of autobiographical expressions and
by naive utterances, especially those which
reveal what he assumes to be obvious and generally taken for granted."

The above indicates that each person in a society is
not subjected to the same cultural environment or to
the same social demands. It represents an early
statement of reference group and role theory, the behavior of the person being a function of the roles he
is expected to play in the groups which he uses as
social referents. The problem posed was how the individual chose his course of action from among those
proposed or demanded by the conflicting or competing
groups. The differential association theory was an
attempt to answer that question.

1-1   THE DIFFERENTIAL ASSOCIATION THEORY

Although Edwin H. Sutherland first incorporated
his differential association theory in the third edition of his *Principles of Criminology* in 1939, the
fourth edition in 1947, the last before his death in
1950, containing a number of changes and revisions,
will be taken here to represent his theory in its final form. The later editions in 1955, 1960, 1966,
and 1970, with Donald R. Cressey as the coauthor,
present us with no innovations in the theory.

In the fourth edition, Sutherland (1947, p. 5-8)
differentiated between the mechanistic and the genetic explanations of crime. The former explains crime
in terms of the factors which are operating at the
moment of the crime. It included the tendencies of
the individual and the nature of the situation in
which he was acting. The situation may involve an
opportunity to steal or to commit some other crime.
A bank may be poorly protected, or an auto may be
parked with the keys in it. The opportunity to steal,
however, only results in theft when the person who
sees the opportunity defines it as an opportunity and

is willing to take advantage of it. His definition
of the situation can only be understood, however,
from the genetic point of view, i.e., in terms of the
actor's life history. Sutherland classified the differential association theory as a genetic explanation
of crime in that it was assumed the criminal act
could occur only when a situation appropriate for it,
as defined by the actor, was present.

There has been some controversy over the differential association theory (Sutherland and Cressey,
1960, p. vi). It is desirable, therefore, to intro-
duce the theory through a statement made by its
author (Sutherland, 1942, p. 20-21) before the Ohio
Valley Sociological Society:

> "First, culture relating to criminal law
> is not uniform or homogeneous in any modern
> society.... (He is assuming culture conflict.)

> "The second concept, differential associa-
> tion, is a statement of culture conflict from
> the point of view of the person who commits
> the crime. The two kinds of culture impinge
> on him and he has associations with the two
> kinds of cultures, and this is differential
> association."

Leaving out the explanatory material, the differential association theory (Sutherland, 1947), p. 6-8)
consists of nine propositions which are:

1. Criminal behavior is learned.
2. Criminal behavior is learned in interaction
   with other persons in a process of communication.
3. The principal part of the learning of criminal behavior occurs within intimate primary groups.
4. When criminal behavior is learned, the
   learning includes (a) techniques of commit-
   ing the crime, which are sometimes compli-
   cated, sometimes very simple; (b) the specific direction of motives, drives, rationalizations, and attitudes.

5. The specific direction of motives and drives is learned from definitions of legal codes as favorable and unfavorable.
6. A person becomes delinquent because of an excess of definitions favorable to violations of law over definitions unfavorable to violations of law. This is the principle of differential association.
7. Differential associations may vary in frequency, duration, priority, and intensity.
8. The process of learning criminal behavior by association with criminal and anticriminal patterns involves all the mechanisms that are involved in any other learning.
9. Though criminal behavior is an expression of general needs and values, it is not explained by those general needs and values, since noncriminal behavior is an expression of the same needs and values.

These nine propositions do not all have the same subject. To paraphrase them, a person becomes criminal by learning criminal behavior patterns, like any other behavior patterns, principally through his interaction with others as a member of one or more intimate groups. It is not so much the learning of the techniques of crime that explain the criminal behavior as it is the learning of motives, drives, rationalizations, and values. Since each person learns attitudes and values which are against as well as for crime, the relative (differential) influence of ideas for or against crime which are operating at a given time will determine whether a person commits a criminal act or not. Of considerable influence on one's judgment or assessment of the situation will be his general attitude toward law observation and law violation.

The theory of differential association deals essentially with the *content* of the learning and not its source. Each person is exposed to criminal and noncriminal cultures, to definitions for and against observance of the law, in differential amounts. Donald Cressey (1960, p. 1), in an analysis of the differential association theory, wrote:

"Sutherland called the process of these definitions (for and against the legal codes) "differential association," because the content of what is learned in association with criminal behavior patterns differs from the content of what is learned in association with anticriminal behavior patterns."

It is erroneous to consider the differential association theory as the differential association of people. Almost everyone presents contradictory definitions of the law, perhaps condemning thieves for violation of the laws of theft and at the same time condemning the police for enforcing certain laws, e.g., traffic and motor vehicle laws, laws with respect to gambling and/or liquor sales. Even the thief supports some of the laws, perhaps those which forbid murder and personal violence, while holding that the laws he violates are a special case. Differential association does not deal with *whom* a person interacts, but with the content of the learning that is imparted, either intentionally or unwittingly.

It is doubtful if the differential association theory can be tested directly with empirical data. DeFleur and Quinney (1960), reformulating the theory in terms of set-theory, concluded that the principal reason for this was the high level of abstraction involved, but they were optimistic that lower order verifiable hypotheses could be derived from it. The general difficulties of testing the differential association theory have also been discussed by Clinard (1959), Short (1960), Cressey (1966), Weinberg (1966), Matthews (1968), and Liska (1969). It is my own view that the difficulty lies primarily in obtaining data with respect to the independent variable, *definitions* favorable and *definitions* unfavorable to law-observance. Although proposition seven indicates that some kind of counting or measuring of these definitions might be obtained, if we take the genetic view which was espoused by Sutherland we have an almost impossible task of recording data during the lifetime of the individual concerned. And if we follow the symbolic-interactionist approach, we have the addi-

tional problem of ascertaining the actor's interpretations of the definitions as they come along through
time. Even Donald Cressey (1966) has to admit that
at present, in terms of the differential association
theory we are unable to predict who will and who will
not become criminal. That, of course, is a weakness
of social science in general, and perhaps all we can
hope for is some kind of probability statement concerning variables as related to crime.

In spite of its empirical weaknesses, the differential association theory does have an undeniable
face validity, in that persons who live in the most
criminal environment where criminal patterns are most
available and numerous are more likely to become criminal than those who live in less criminal environments. It has been pointed out, for example, that
the boy who grows up in a deteriorated slum area has
a greater chance of becoming a member of a delinquent
gang than a boy who is reared in a middle-class neighborhood. There, as a member of a delinquent gang, he
is exposed to a considerable number of delinquent and
criminal patterns, and as a result he is more likely
to become delinquent than is the middle-class boy
(Cressey, 1960, p. 3; Glaser, 1960, p. 6-7). Persons
who serve time in penal institutions live in a relatively homogeneous criminal environment, so far as
attitudes toward the law are concerned, and these persons are more likely to get into difficulty with the
law after their release than others who, though criminal, are given a different treatment than confinement (Glaser, 1960, p. 8). There is also considerable evidence that boys who are members of delinquent
gangs are relatively isolated from conventional noncriminal patterns (Glaser, 1960, p. 8). They are
less likely to spend time at home, at school, or at
settlement houses. Part of this isolation is voluntary, but part of it is due to their rejection from
conventional circles by those who object to their
conduct. In actual application, the differential
association theory has become the group delinquency
theory, since it is assumed that it is the group
(gang) that is the carrier of the delinquent patterns.

The theory of differential association was first used by Edwin H. Sutherland to explain systematic crime, or crime engaged in by persons who make crime their career. Later he extended it to all forms of crime, and even to a category of crime which he called "white-collar crime," which we will here rough- ly define as crime committed by an upper-class person as part of his business or professional activity, mostly by violation of a delegated or implied trust. Prime examples of white-collar criminals are the "robber barons," such as Kreuger, Whitney, Insull, Fall, Sinclair, and others. These "criminals" did not become members of juvenile gangs in their youth, but they learned about crime nonetheless:

> "Those who become white-collar criminals generally start their careers in good neigh- borhoods and good homes, graduate from col- leges with some idealism, and, with little selection on their part, get into particular business situations in which criminality is practiced as a folkway, and are inducted into that system of behavior just as into any other folkway" (Sutherland, 1940, p. 10-11).

It is suggested here that the theory of differen- tial association, dealing mostly with folkways and patterns which are differentially observed and assimi- lated by various segments of our population, has made an important contribution to the thesis that crime in general is the result of social and cultural influ- ences. However, it does not sufficiently get down to the level of the actor, his perspective, and his atti- tudes. The differential identification theory is a step in that direction.

1-2   THE DIFFERENTIAL IDENTIFICATION THEORY

Using the language of symbolic-interaction psy- chology, Daniel Glaser (1956) defines first "identi- fication" and then "differential identification" as follows:

"The image of behavior as role-playing, borrowed from the theater, presents people as directing their actions on the basis of conceptions of how others see them. The choice of another, from whose perspective we view our behavior, is the process of identification.

"The theory of differential identification, in essence, is that a person pursues criminal behavior to the extent that he identifies himself with real or imaginary persons from whose perspective his criminal behavior is acceptable."

The theory of differential identification focuses attention on the interaction in which choice of role-models occurs. It is consistent with the idea that a great deal of criminality is learned from others who support one or more types of criminal behavior, but it also allows for the fact that one may identify with and be influenced by persons with whom one is not in direct contact. It recognizes that the identifications one makes grow out of experiences, but that behavior changes may be due to changing situations. And finally, it assumes that the behavior of others can be changed by somehow altering their identifications. Instead of focusing on the patterns of criminal and noncriminal behavior in one's immediate social environment, it focuses on the relationship of an actor to those persons with whom he identifies.

1-3   REFERENCE GROUPS DEFINED

There are three general definitions of reference groups: comparative, status, and normative reference groups (Shibutani, 1955, p. 563). We will define each before developing a composite definition.

Comparative reference group. A comparative reference group is a group with which one compares himself in making a self-judgment. Herbert Hyman (1942), who is generally credited with first studying reference groups, was interested in how people judged

their own status. He found their judgment was largely accomplished by comparing themselves with others,
whom he designated as either reference individuals or
as reference groups. The status a person accorded
himself was ascertained, Hyman found, relative to the
choice of the person or persons with whom he compared
himself. This conception of reference group is also
found in the writings of Robert K. Merton (1957, p.
229-259), especially as it applied to the concept of
relative deprivation. The latter concept indicates
that a person tends to compare himself with others
who share the same situation with him or who possess
the same status attributes (sex, race, marital status,
education, etc.) in deciding whether to feel pleased
or unhappy over some experience. For example, public
opinion surveys conducted during World War II found
that soldiers who were married were more unhappy over
being drafted than soldiers who were single. This
was attributed by the army research group to the fact
that married men in general were seldom drafted but
single men were frequently drafted. Those married
men who were drafted, therefore, felt more discrimin-
ated against than the single men.

In a discussion of reference groups, Theodore
Kemper (1968) enlarged on the functions of the comparative reference group. It provides the actor with a
frame of reference:

> "... which serves to facilitate judgments
> about any of several problematic issues, viz.:
> (a) the equity of one's fate; (b) the legiti-
> macy of one's actions and attitudes; (c) the
> adequacy of one's performance; or (d) the
> accommodation of one's acts to the acts of
> others."

Category (c) relates to the fact that one uses a role
model to evaluate one's progress in a role as well as
to learn the role. In discussing the lack of ambition among certain lower-class blacks, Kemper intro-
duces the idea of their lack of adequate role models:

> "For even adequate role performance to oc-
> cur, a role model is required. A major prob-

lem in the lower class Negro community, both
where the family is intact and where it is not,
is that the depressed state of Negro attainment, combined with the ghetto living that
makes society's high attainers, i.e., whites,
both visible and disliked, deprive growing
Negro youth of role models."

In terms of reference group theory, one does not need
to be in direct social contact with his reference
group (role model) in order to be influenced by it,
but it helps. Kemper also calls our attention to the
fact that one's reference group not only provides him
with the model for appropriate behavior, but also
with a model which exemplifies those attitudes which
are desirable.

Status reference group. The second definition
of reference group is that it is a group in which the
actor seeks acceptance. He may want acceptance into
a group to which he does not presently belong, or he
may wish to have a relatively high or favorable position in a group to which he presently belongs.

Normative reference group. A reference group
has also been defined as a group whose values, norms,
and perspective the actor uses in defining a social
situation. The norms and values in question may be
those of conventional society or some deviant group,
category, or collectivity.

It should be clear that in a given situation the
same group may serve the function of a person's comparative, status, and normative reference group, but
Albert Cohen and James Short (1961) point out that
this is not always the case. A boy may want to be
accepted by his parents, but follow the norms of his
gang or vice versa.

A Definition of Reference Groups

In discussing different types of reference
groups, Ralph Turner (1961, p. 327) observed that it

is somewhat immaterial whether we define a reference
group from the status or the normative standpoint.
One who focuses on the normative content and its im-
port to the individual may use the normative conception of reference groups; one who focuses on the mech-
anism by which the normative content is acquired will
use the status conception of reference groups. Basically, they are inseparable. It remained for Muzafer
and Carolyn Sherif (1964, p. 180) to put these two
conceptions of a reference group into one definition:

> "Those groups in which he wants to be
> counted as an individual which include the
> individuals whose opinions make a difference
> for him, whose standards and goals are his,
> are his reference group."

This definition makes sense, because every group in
which a person seeks acceptance requires implicitly
or explicitly as a condition of acceptance as a member in good standing that he must accept its norms,
standards, and values. The statement by Gouldner and
Gouldner (1963, p. 320):

> "The stronger the motivation to stay in the
> group and the greater its attraction and its
> rewards, the more he will adapt his beliefs,
> values and behavior to the group's norms."

is well documented by reference to Back (1951),
Schachter (1951), Kelley and Volkart (1952), and Emerson (1954).

Not only is identification with or acceptance of
a group tantamount to acceptance of its norms, but it
is equally true that the acceptance of any set of
norms or standards implies recognition of some group
which supports them.

The literature on reference groups mentions positive and negative reference groups (Newcomb, 1950, p.
226; Merton, 1957, p. 320). In both cases the actor
accepts the viewpoint of the other while taking his
role. If he accepts the norms and appraisal of the

other, it is a positive reference group. If he rejects the norms and appraisal of the other, it is a
negative reference group. Mizruchi (1964, p. 21) mentions the beatnik as a person who enjoys the rejection of others, making the inference that since he
engages in behavior that he knows is disapproved by
conventional society, that he is actively seeking society's condemnation. The same might be said of the
criminal whose illegal activities set him at odds
with the rest of the community. Both inferences are
wrong because they relate the actor to the wrong reference group. Although a person may respond negative-
ly to a group and/or its values, it seems to the
writer that the definition of reference group he is
accepting is inconsistent with the concept of negative reference group. If one accepts the members of
his reference group and their norms, how can he reject the group whose acceptance he wants or the norms
which he accepts as his own?

1-4   CLASSES OF REFERENCE GROUPS

According to Robert Merton (1957, p. 284), the
term "reference group" is really a misnomer, because
the actor may obtain a self-judgment not only from a
group but also from a collectivity, a category of persons, and an individual. Each of these will be considered in turn.

Groups. Frederick Thrasher, Clifford Shaw, and
Edwin H. Sutherland dealt particularly with the boy's
gang as the source of many of the attitudes and illegal behavior of the boys who made up the juvenile
gang. These gangs provided a set of values and norms
in terms of which the boys judged one another and
themselves. The term "gang" meets the definition of
a group, which is a number of persons who interact
with one another according to established patterns
(or roles), share a common code or set of values and
norms, define themselves as members who have certain
rights and duties with respect to one another, and
are thought of by outsiders as belonging to the group
(Merton, 1957, p. 284-6).

It is recognized that the boundaries of a group are to some extent fixed, so that it is known who is in and who is not, but the boundary may vary with the situation, especially if the group is an informal one. For some purposes a gang may consist of half a dozen members, and for other purposes it may have a score or more. Under some conditions a juvenile delinquent gang is referred to as a "near-group." It is then characterized by diffused role definition, limited cohesion, impermanence, minimal consensus of norms, shifting membership, disturbed leadership, and limited clarity on group objectives (Yablonsky, 1959). The near-group is most likely to be formed with the attributes of a mob when the juveniles of one neighborhood battle with those of another.

Collectivities. A reference group constitutes a collectivity when those who make it up

> "... have a sense of solidarity by virtue of sharing common values and who have acquired an attendant sense of moral obligation to fulfill role expectations" (Merton, 1947, p. 299).

This concept does not have the requirement of interaction found in that of the group, but the group may be considered a subcategory of collectivity in that its members have solidarity, common orientations, and a moral obligation to fulfill certain roles. Examples of collectivities are unorganized individuals who belong to the underworld, who have an interest in the same hobby, who pursue the same sport. They feel a kinship through the pursuit of their common values rather than through interaction.

Social categories. The people who constitute a reference group may also be those who do not have *common* values nor engage in interaction, but who have similar interests and values by virtue of the fact that they fall into the same status category. Thus people may feel some identification with others who have the same sex, race, age, marital status, or criminal record, and who, therefore, share commonali-

ties in their roles. It is for this reason that
groups are frequently formed from the persons who
share the same status category and that identification with a given status category is sometimes one of
the prerequisites for membership in a group.

Perhaps one of the reasons for the *success* of
Alcoholics Anonymous lies in the fact that social
groups are formed out of those with the same status
category--alcoholics. Thus they come to have common
and reciprocal roles instead of similar interests as
they face the problem of drinking. Conversely, the
failure of reformatories and prisons can be partly
traced to the fact that those who are given the same
status by the courts--convicted offenders--are housed
together under conditions which encourage those of
the same status to become a collectivity or group.

Reference individual. In a study of organized
crime in Chicago in the late 1920's John Landesco
(1929) provides us with a description of the attitude
of the youthful gangster toward the underworld leaders:

"He speaks in flowing admiration of the
power, the courage, the skill, the display and
the generosity of the outstanding gang leaders.
His glorification of the life and the character of the underworld is complete evidence of
the absence of any feeling of inferiority or
shame about his criminal aspirations. The
following statement by a gambler and confidence man is representative of the attitude
of the majority of criminals:

"'The men of the underworld are the brain-
iest in the world. They have to be, because
they live by their wits. They are always
planning something, a 'stick-up,' a burglary,
or some new 'racket.' They are constantly in
danger. They have to think quicker and sharp-
er than the other fellow. They have to 'size
up' every man they meet, and figure out what
'line' to use on him. The leading men of the
underworld can move in every circle of society.

They are at home in Chinatown, along the 'main
stem,' in gambling dives, or in the best ho-
tels of the 'Gold Coast.' When they have a
lucky 'break' they can live like million-
aires; when their money is spent they plan new
schemes.'"

We also find Clifford Shaw (1933, p. 87) making
reference to reference individuals:

"The criminal group has its heroes, its
'big shots,' its prominent persons who have
gained prestige and power in the delinquent
world. Such persons are well-known in the
delinquency areas of the city and are often
emulated by the younger members of delinquent
groups. To the young delinquent, the 'big
shot' symbolizes success and power in the
criminal world and represents an ideal to be
achieved."

In the book, *Brothers in Crime*, Shaw (1938, p.
345) continues with:

"Usually the boys who are most habituated
and sophisticated in stealing are the ones who
are most advantageously situated for trans-
mitting information about delinquency to other
boys. By virtue of greater experience in delinquency, they often occupy positions of superior status and prestige. Thus they are emulated, idolized, and respected. The beginners
are especially receptive to their influence
and instruction...."

The reference group may be a single person who
serves as his ideal or model. When identification
with the other relates to more than one of his roles,
Merton (1957, p. 302) refers to the other as a reference individual; if identification is with respect to
but one role, he is referred to as a role-model. The
primary significance of this distinction, it seems to
me, is that it calls attention to the fact that the
more one knows about one's ideal the more he will be
influenced by him.

Significant others. Shibutani (1961, p. 339) defines "significant others" as those persons who are
of crucial importance for the construction and reinforcement of one's self-conception. They represent,
therefore, a type of reference group.

1-5   IMPLICATIONS OF THE CONCEPT
OF REFERENCE GROUP

The concept of reference group is particularly
helpful in bringing out the fact that each individual
in our heterogeneous society is in social interaction
with a diversity of persons, each of whom makes somewhat contradictory demands upon him (Muzafer Sherif,
1953, p. 204). It reminds us that the individual is
responding to a variety of values and personal influences as he meets this situation and that. Each reference group has its own set of norms and values,
which may include influences for or against criminal
behavior. Each reference group with which a person
is in interaction has sanctions with which it endeavors to further its own norms, values, and interests.
Contradictory or conflicting demands by those in his
role-set or status-set (see Chapter 2) require some
kind of selection on the part of the actor, and those
whose point of view he takes in making his selection
are his reference group.

It is easy enough to see how a person who grew
up in a delinquent neighborhood and associated almost
exclusively with delinquents would select delinquents
and criminals as his reference group, and take their
norms and values as his own. We expect people to
think and act like those of their own group. What
reference group theory adds to that commonplace observation is an allowance for the fact that one does not
need to have direct contact with a group in order to
be influenced by it. Reference group theory takes
into account the fact that one can be influenced by a
group without becoming a member of it, and one can
become a delinquent or criminal without growing up in
a delinquent neighborhood (Merton, 1957, p. 282).

1-6   IDENTIFICATION OF REFERENCE GROUPS

Robert K. Merton refers to two types of reference groups: membership groups and nonmembership
groups, the distinction resting upon whether the actor is in fact a member of that collectivity or not
(Merton, 1957), p. 236). One may, for example, use
as his reference group a club or an organization to
which he aspires but into which he has not yet been
admitted. He may also engage in anticipatory socialization, following the norms of the groups to which he
aspires. This means that one cannot identify another's reference groups by merely observing those with
whom the other is interacting. In fact, it might be
misleading. While the robber is clearly interacting
with the victim, he is in all probability using as
his reference group persons who are absent from the
scene but who approve of robbery. In actual life we
sometimes get around the difficulty of identifying
the reference groups of persons engaged in conflict,
or where the behavior of one person is not supported
by the others who are present, by identifying the
actor's norms and values, and then ascribing them to
some reference group which shares these norms and values. This means that valid research concerning a person's reference group usually requires the cooperation of the subject, who either (a) supplies information directly about his values, ideals, role models,
status ambitions, and the like which constitute elements of the reference group he is using, or (b) provides the verbal data from which a skilled therapist
can infer the use of reference groups of which the
subject is himself unaware.

2. HOW REFERENCE GROUPS INFLUENCE BEHAVIOR

Herbert Kelman (1961) has described three processes by which persons respond to social influence:
compliance, identification, and internalization.
They provide us with some very useful analytic tools
for dealing with the influence of reference groups.

Compliance occurs when an individual accepts
influence from another person or group in order to
achieve a desired response from the other. He does
what he thinks the other wants in order to achieve
some reward and/or avoid an undesirable cost. It depends upon the power of the other to influence the actor's outcome, that is, his rewards minus his costs,
and upon the alternative choices that the actor sees
open to him.

Identification occurs when a person accepts an
influence from another in order to establish and maintain a desirable relationship with the other, thereby
achieving a satisfactory self-conception or identity.
The relationship may be either with an individual to
whom one is attracted or with a group to which his
self-definition is anchored. To have his identity
validated he must meet the expectations of his fellows, i.e., accept their influence. As it applies to
delinquency, Clifford Shaw (1933) has written:

> "It is a matter of general observation
> that individuals are most sensitive to the
> attitudes of approval and disapproval of

those with whom they are most intimately associated or those who belong to their own club,
sect, social class, or profession. The delinquent is no exception to the rule. He is much
more responsive to the opinions and judgments
of his companions in crime, or to the members
of the criminal class in general, than he is
to the larger society. He seeks to secure the
esteem and approbation of his fellows by con-
ducting himself in a manner acceptable to his
group."

It is through the process of identification that
many of our norms and values are assimilated. One is
not only influenced to do what the other wants but
also to think as the other does. In a study of primary group influence on party loyalty, McClosky and
Dahlgren (1964, p. 209) conclude:

"The belief that people who associate together come to think alike is now so thorough-
ly buttressed by research and daily observation that it has become a commonplace. Studies have shown that the more intimately we relate to our associates, the greater the cor-
respondence between their views and ours.
Since we interact most frequently and famil-
iarly with the members of our own primary
group, it is mainly in these groups that our
social and political attitudes are anchored."

One may also add that it is in these groups that our
attitudes toward lawful behavior are anchored. The
further significance of the primary group in the shaping of attitudes, and in the assimilation of norms
and values, is reiterated in the literature of sociology, and so needs no further corroboration.

Internalization occurs when one accepts an influence because it is congruent with his value system.
The content of the behavior or idea is intrinsically
rewarding because it is congenial to the actor's
value system, and is, in fact, demanded by his value
system. It is, of course, recognized that internali-

zation must be preceded by the process of identification. It is hoped by street gang workers that
through the process of identification with the worker,
and the development of dependence upon him, that the
gang boys will come to accept the goals and norms of
conventional society (Spergel, 1965, p. 83), and sub-
sequently to accept only those influences congenial
to his new value system.

These three processes--compliance, identification, and internalization--are not mutually exclusive,
but frequently overlap. For analytic purposes, the
goal in compliance is to achieve an effect, in identification to achieve or maintain a social relationship,
and in internalization to make one's own values congruent. Kelman's description of compliance indicates
that it refers chiefly to overt behavior, with little
or no change in private attitudes. Identification
relates generally to the status aspect and internalization to the normative aspect of reference groups.
We will take up the status and normative aspects of
reference groups separately, keeping in mind, however,
that in real life they are inseparable.

2-1   THE STATUS ASPECT OF REFERENCE
GROUP BEHAVIOR

Reference groups influence behavior in a given
setting by (a) defining for the actor his self-
conception, self-identity, or social type, (b) specifying the roles or norms appropriate for one such as
he, (c) observing his role performance, and (d) exercising appropriate sanctions (rewards or costs),
thereby affecting the actor's satisfactions, including his self-image.

Self-identity. A person must know who he is before he can tell which roles or behavior are appropriate for him. He identifies himself in relation to
(a) other people and/or (b) positions in the social
structure. He defines himself in terms of groups or
groupings to which he belongs, or hopes to belong,
and his position in each if he is a member. He may

also operationally define his location in social
terms by describing or naming the role or roles he is
expected to play.

Andrew Wade (1967) in a study of juvenile vandalism came to the conclusion that:

> "The participant's self-image is ... of
> prime importance. This includes his defini-
> tion of the act of vandalism as essentially a
> 'prank' or a 'good joke' on the victim or vic-
> tims. Certain rationalizations are utilized
> to make possible this self-definition. These
> tend to neutralize any guilt feelings present
> as a consequence of the internalization of the
> cultural norms governing the sanctity and
> worth of personal and public property. Also
> included are the over-all attitudes the ado-
> lescent has toward himself, toward juvenile
> behavior in general, and toward the reactions
> of peers to deviant behavior in general....
>
> "The juvenile's conception of the act of
> vandalism is a clue to his self-image. If he
> construes the event as 'just a joke' or 'just
> having fun,' it implies that he thinks of him-
> self as a 'prankster' and not specifically as
> a delinquent."

The importance of one's self-image is in large
measure a function of how others view one. There is
a body of theory in the area of deviance, epitomized
by Howard Becker's (1963) *The Outsiders*, which con-
tends that society makes its own deviants by labeling
people as such. The deviant is not only accorded an
inferior status, which affects his self-evaluation,
but he is also avoided by conventionally oriented persons, and thereby forced into the arms of others who
share his label. While persons with good reputations
avoid deviant acts to escape the stigma of the deviant label, those who are in fact so labeled are pro-
grammed by society into the kind of persons society
thinks them to be.

The greater the number of significant others who
are perceived to define an aspect of a person's self-

conception congruently, the more that aspect of his self is resistant to change (Backman, et al., 1963, p. 168). Without a congruent and stable view of one's self, maintained by a stable set of social ties, roles, and commitments, an individual is subject to feelings of anxiety and apathy. In a study of systematic bad check writers, Edwin Lemert (1967, p. 126-7) reports the difficulty this type of offender encounters in trying to establish and maintain an identity by reference to purely extrinsic rewards:

"To admit this (difficulty) is for the forger in effect to admit that the roles he plays, or his way of life, makes impossible a stable identity or the validation of a self-ideal. An excerpt from an older published autobiography of a forger states the problem clearly.

"'I could not rid myself of the crying need for the sense of security which social recognition and contact with one's fellows, and their approval furnishes. I was lonely and frightened and wanted to be where there was someone who knew me as I had been before.'

"At best the forger can seek to use his affluence to buy from others the approval and recognition important to a sense of personal worth. But persons endowed with the intelligence and insight of a systematic check criminal quickly perceive the spurious qualities of such esteem, founded only on his generosity.

"'Sure, you get big money. But it's easy come, easy go. You start out on Monday morning with a stack of checks. Maybe it's hard to get started, but after the first check it's easier. You work all week and by Thursday or Friday you have a pocketful of money. Then you pick up a girl and hit the bars and night spots. You have plenty of quick pals to pat you on the back and help you spend that money. Pretty soon it's Monday morning and you wake up with a hangover and empty pockets. You need more money so you start again.'

"... The forger, by choice, enacts the form
but not the substance of social roles. He
lacks, avoids, or rejects contact with reference groups which would validate these roles
or fix an underlying identity. He cannot par-
ticularize his social interaction, hence he
has no way of getting appreciation as a separate person. Appreciation must remain super-
ficial imputations to the persons whose real
or hypothetical identities he assumes. Apart
from the lack of opportunity to do so, the
forger dares not put too much of what he re-
gards as his 'true self' into these identities;
he cannot readily convert them and make them
his own either in part or in whole. To par-
ticularize his interaction to such an end
would disclose his essential difference from
others, i.e., his commitment to living by pass-
ing bogus check and deceiving others. This
disclosure, of course, would destroy the identities or assign him the criminal identity
which he does not desire."

A person's identity is not just who he is, but
what he wants to be, his ambitions and goals. The
latter are determined largely by his reference group,
according to Ralph H. Turner (1964, p. 129-30):

"Reference group theory has suggested two
important ways in which groups affect an individual's ambition. One way is in the deter-
mination and selection of goals, according to
the objects which are valued in the reference
group. Identification with the group and its
prestigeful members inclines the member toward
adoption of the goals which are conspicuously
held by them....

"The other reference group process has to
do with the setting of standards rather than
goals. Goals such as material, occupational,
and educational success are continua. Two
persons may value material success, but their
conceptions of how much wealth constitutes
success may be quite different. 'Goal' refers

to the direction of ambition; 'standard' refers to the level of attainment which is re-
garded as success. Standards are set partly
by the same processes we have described for
goals. But they are also set by the process
of comparing oneself with others. The question, 'How far is up?' is answered in relation
to how far others are known to have ascended.
One may set his standards by reference to public figures and groups, but we suspect that
standards are more often based upon individuals and groups who are close at hand.... This
standard-setting by comparison with a reference group is supplemented by the group's ef-
fects upon courage and opportunity to learn
the means for ascent. Ambition always con-
tains an element of risk. The evidence that
others like oneself hold the same ambitions,
is a source of courage to take the necessary
risk. Ambition also implies some assessment
of the means. Persons who have immediate contact with other people who have achieved a
given level are more likely to feel that they
understand how to get there and consequently
are willing to set their standards accordingly."

In his book, *Heroes, Villains, and Fools,* Orrin
E. Klapp (1962) described a kind of self-identity
which he calls social typing. It involves a pigeon-
holing of people, including one's self. One may
think of himself as a hero to be followed, a villain
to be avoided as dangerous, or a fool who falls ludi-
crously short of a social norm. Other social types
are fast talkers, do-gooders, boosters, good fellows,
operators, tough guys, and the like. The social type
one sees himself as fitting are pseudo reference
groups, form part of one's self-conception, and affect his choice of associates.

"The self-type is a major clue to a man's
character: he will reject the suggestions
and memberships inconsistent with it and prefer those which build it up; phrases such as
he 'cramps my style,' 'makes me sick,' or

'brings out my better side,' 'indicates that
the individual is seeking associates who will
let him be the kind of self he wants to be"
(Klapp, 1962, p. 22).

In a somewhat similar vein, Alex Inkeles in discussing child socialization wrote:

"From the standpoint of the individual,
knowing his identity seems to be a psychological requirement for personal integration....
It is only by knowing 'who he is'--that is by
knowing his status and role--that he discrim-
inates between the massive flow of stimuli
from others and selects only those signals to
which he must pay attention and perhaps respond, according to his position in the system
of interaction" (Inkeles, 1968, p. 122).

It is in line with this theme that Reckless,
Dinitz, and Murray (1956) concluded from their study
of nondelinquents in a delinquent neighborhood that
the nondelinquents' conception of themselves as "good
boys" insulated them from the norms, values, and behavior patterns of the delinquent boys who lived
nearby.

Scott Briar and Irving Piliavin (1965) include
the self-concept in their analysis of delinquency.
They argue that negative explanations of nondelin-
quency are basically weak when put in terms of constraints provided by (a) the norms of the larger
society, (b) the internalized parental prohibitions
and demands, or (c) the formal institutions of society. As a substitute, they stress the central processes of social control in a positive fashion as "commitments to conformity":

"By this term we mean not only fear of the
material deprivations and punishments which
might result from being discovered as an offender but also apprehension about the dele-
terious consequences of such a discovery on
one's attempts to maintain a consistent self-

image, to sustain value relationships, and to preserve current and future statuses and activities" (Briar and Piliavin, 1965, p. 39).

The driving force is seen as oriented to a future gain, rather than avoidance of a loss.

The concept of "commitment to conformity" is consistent with reference group theory which recognizes the importance of a person's self-image and his relationship to significant others. It is also consistent with the symbolic interactionists observation that the on-going social act is related to the goals toward which the individual is oriented. Opening up of job opportunities have little effect, Briar and Piliavin point out, until the boy has reached the age when jobs are desired. It is in terms of goals that opportunities are seized and utilized.

The positive thrust of a person's goals can also be seen in Albert Cohen's article, "The Sociology of the Deviant Act" (1965) in which it is pointed out that although we may see the offender as a deviant, from the actor's viewpoint he may be a conformist:

"A tough and bellicose posture, the use of obscene language, participation in illicit sexual activity, the immoderate consumption of alcohol, the deliberate flouting of legality and authority, a generalized disrespect for the sacred symbols of the 'square world,' a taste for marijuana, even suicide--all of these may have the primary function of affirming, in the language of gesture and deed, that one is a certain kind of person" (Cohen, 1965, p. 13).

The Reckless, et al. (1956) study suggests that a person's reference group can be thought of as either an independent or as a dependent variable. It is independent when it offers him a favorable self-identity in return for his compliance to its norms or an unfavorable self-identity for noncompliance. The parents of a boy can penalize him by calling him a "bad boy," and the gang can penalize him by calling him a "square" or "sissy." On the other hand, the individual is not a passive actor, but can contribute to the stability of his self-identity by choosing an interpersonal environment which is congruent with his self-concept and his behavior. This is sometimes achieved by such devices as (a) misperceiving the attitudes of others toward himself, (b) interacting principally with persons whose attitudes are congruent with his own and who support his self-conception, (c) acting in such a way that he validates the identity he desires, and (d) holding to those images of himself that fit his idealized self while discarding images of himself that are not flattering (Secord and Backman, 1964, p. 596).

Roles and norms. A person's identity ties him in with some reference group and a set of norms appropriate to the status with which he is identified. In order for a person to have or use a reference group he must at least vaguely know which reference group he is using and what the norms of that group are (Norman Kaplan, 1955). The accuracy of his perception of the norms and values of a group will largely be a function of the extent to which he had direct contact with it. In discussing nonmembership groups Robert K. Merton refers to "anticipatory socialization" as the process by which a person acquires the norms and values of a group prior to his acceptance into it. The problem of the mobile individual and his reference group was investigated by Ralph H. Turner ("Upward Mobility and Class Values," 1964, p. 360), who found:

> "The values which the individual internalizes because of his positive attraction to the group are not necessarily those which careful investigation would ascribe to the group, but express his image of the group. His image may reflect the perspectives of his socializing agents, such as parent, teacher, or uncle, who have taught him to value the group. It may consist in part of a fantasy which is in contrast to disturbing aspects of his contemporary

membership situation. Or it may be distorted
by the selective opportunities available to
him for observing the group's expression of
values."

We must not assume that a person learns the
norms of status X only from the membership of the organization in which status X is located. A family,
for example, can tell one of its members who is newly
recruited into the army what his obligations to the
army are. It frequently happens that one institution
will support the norms of another institution. More
than one reference group may exert pressure upon an
individual to perform a given role in a specified way.

Observation of role performance. Reference
groups not only define a person's identity and speci-
fy the roles appropriate for him, but they also tend
to monitor or observe his role performance to see if
he complies with their expectations or not. When the
reference groups to which a person is oriented in his
various roles and statuses disagree with respect to
their expectations concerning his appropriate behavior, he experiences what is called role conflict
(Seemans, 1953, p. 373; Laulicht, 1955, p. 250).

Merton (1957) has described various ways in
which people customarily solve the problem of role
conflict, such as (a) giving priority to role demands
upon the basis of some socially recognized precedence
rating, (b) recognizing the demand of the group with
the greatest power, (c) turning the problem over to
those making the demands to settle the issue among
themselves, (d) getting others to sympathize with him
upon the basis that they too have role conflicts, and
(e) simply avoiding confrontation through secrecy and
compartmentalization of various areas of their lives.
It is the latter solution that delinquents are most
likely to turn to, since the other solutions are not
likely to be acceptable to reference groups that have
a law-abiding outlook.

An obvious effect of the offender hiding his de-
linquencies from law-abiding reference groups is the

greater power which this gives to the law-violating reference groups. They are in a position to monitor and direct his behavior, and to exact penalties for deviance from their norms, while the law-abiding groups are left in darkness and relative weakness. The matters that law-violating groups cannot monitor about their members are basically immaterial to them; the matters that the law-abiding groups cannot monitor about their members may be crucially important to them.

We must not conclude that delinquents and criminals are at odds with conventional society in all areas of their lives. There are many areas of agreement, generally including the recognition that a man has a social responsibility toward his wife, children, and kin. Even the professional criminal sees the good sense in abiding by most of our laws, since to violate even a traffic law is to draw attention to himself. The sophisticated offender adheres to most of the social norms, violating the law only when the risk is low and/or the rewards are sufficiently high.

It is to be expected that a person considering whether or not to violate a given norm will subjectively evaluate the probability of the norm violation being observed and acted upon by others. This is true even of most conformists. As Briar and Piliavin (1965, p. 39) point out:

> "Even persons with strong commitments to conformity experience motives to engage in criminal acts, and they may perform such acts when their commitments do not appear to be threatened (for example, under conditions of low visibility) or when the motives to deviate are very strong."

An example of this may be the occasional college student who is arrested for shoplifting an object which he could afford to buy. No doubt he does not expect to get caught, believing his act to be beyond the vision of others. Had he felt his self-image and his future academic and professional careers threatened

by his impulse to steal, in all likelihood he would
not have taken the risk. This brings up the topic of
sanctions to which we now turn.

Sanctions. As used here, a sanction is the contingent reaction of alter to ego's action (Parsons
and Shils, 1951, p. 15). The reaction of alter may
be in the form of a reward, a punishment, or a combin-
ation of them. Rewards may be thought of as (a) as-
sisting ego in the gratification of his physical
needs and (b) social approval through which ego is
able to secure a more satisfactory self-image and
attendant self-satisfaction. Punishment may consist
in (a) denial of gratification, such as refusal to
perform some service which ego requires and (b) disapproval, which has a tendency to lower ego's sense
of well-being.

The sanctions of a reference group will depend
upon whether that reference group is a group, a collectivity, a social category, or an individual. It
is assumed that only persons with whom an individual
interacts can impose sanctions on him, but some allowance must be made for the fact that the anticipation of sanctions as well as sanctions actually carried out can exert an influence on him. In a psychological sense, ego can experience sanctions from
any reference group, including those that are imaginary.

In an *organized group* the good members uphold
the group values and norms, reacting violently to
deviates and nonconformers (Sherif and Cantril, 1947,
p. 321). They may consider it besides the point that
while violating their norms, ego was conforming to
the norms of another group. There is an unlimited
number of sanctions which a group may impose, of
which a few are withdrawal of approval, refusal to
validate ego's claim to a desired status, changes in
the number and/or kind of rewards for services, changes of ego's ranking in the group, isolation, ejection
from the group, and in extreme cases, corporal or
capital punishment.

Among the various groups to which a person belongs, the primary group is strategically situated to
be an effective reference group:

> "... the members of a primary group enjoy
> unparalleled opportunities to make their atti-
> tudes known, to check, modify, and correct
> each others views, and to bring dissenters in-
> to line. Their power is further augmented by
> their extraordinary capacity for rewarding
> conformity and punishing deviation, and what
> is equally important, for doing so immediately,
> directly, and tangibly" (McClosky and Dahlgren,
> 1964, p. 210).

Furthermore, it is within the primary group that one
is most likely to empathize with the other so that
one becomes more keenly aware of the hurt that the
other feels when ego violates the group norm, and he
is more vulnerable to the opinions they have of him.

I have Ralph H. Turner to thank for calling my
attention to the fact that sentiments of love and
norms of consideration at times inhibit the primary
group from exercising sanctions upon its members for
norm violations. Parents may put up with behavior of
their children that no impersonal group would toler-
ate for a moment. One of the problems of imposing
sanctions within a primary group is that sanctions
may damage positive sentiments of the other, so that
the punisher suffers along with the punished.

Turning now to sanctions for violations of norms
of collectivities and social categories, we may observe that for the most part the sanction involves a
status or self-identity change for the norm violator.
Those who violate good sportmanship norms may be
called "poor sports," inconsiderate motorists are
labeled "road hogs," and those who fail to accept the
legitimacy of gratification norms may be referred to
as "squares." Violators of norms for *social categories* may be denied their claim to the identity whose
norms have been violated: effeminate men may become
"sissies," unlady-like girls referred to as "tomboys,"

and whites who fail to show sufficient solidarity with their race may be derogated as "nigger lovers." Of course, these terms have their desirable counter-terms which are used to reward the actor for his conformity. Changing of a person's identification with a given collectivity or social category raise or lower a person's relative status in the group in which he interacts, so that group sanctions are frequently the consequence of violation of collectivity and social category norms.

The violation of the norms of one's *reference individual* will usually bring repercussions only if the norm violation is observed and the actor is personally acquainted with his reference individual and/or others who are aware of his ideal and let him know how far short of his ideal he has fallen. In the case where the reference individual is a friend the sanctions employed will have the same range as we mentioned in our discussion of group sanctions. If ego and alter constitute a two-person group, the ejection of one means the destruction of the group. If ego and alter are part of the same group, the sanction may include the loss of friendship along with the penalties exercised by the whole group.

2-2   THE NORMATIVE ASPECT OF REFERENCE GROUP BEHAVIOR

The emphasis in the discussion of status reference groups was upon conformity to the expectations of the group in order to secure a desirable status and self-identity. The stress will now be upon the individual's efforts to guide his behavior in terms of the norms and values which he has assimilated from his reference groups. Instead of asking, "Would Joe Blow approve of me and keep me in the gang if I do such and such," the normative problem is, "What is the *rule* or the *value* that applies here, and is it consistent with the set of norms and values I already have," or the question, "Are my standards of behavior validated by the standards of my fellows?"

The distinction between the status and normative aspects of reference group behavior is frequently academic rather than pragmatic in that the individual tends to come out with the same guides to behavior by following either avenue. If Jim Smith wants to know whether Joe Blow would approve of certain conduct or not he asks himself what the norms and values of Joe Blow are, and from them makes his judgment. And to the extent that Joe Blow is a reference individual for Jim Smith, both Joe and Jim will be operating from the same set of values. There are perhaps instances, however, in which Jim will want to influence Joe favorably to gain some desired end, but he is not willing to accept most of Joe's standards and norms. (This is Kelman's influence by compliance.) It may reach the point where Jim has to choose between living by certain principles or going along with the crowd. It is here contended that if Jim chooses to follow principles in this case, he is using a reference group different from the one of which he is a member or in which he is presently interacting.

As used here, the term "normative" behavior refers not only to behavior guided by social norms, including the expected behavior of the roles a person is identified with, but also values and beliefs which support those norms. The essential distinction between values and social norms is that the social norm provides a rule or a description of expected behavior, whereas values provide the criteria in terms of which behavior is evaluated (Vander Zanden, 1965, p. 65). Values define what is good, moral, beautiful, and worthwhile. Some important values in the general American society are achievement, productive work, humanitarianism, rationality, freedom, equality, democracy, and patriotism. Each of them is realized through adherence to a set of social norms. Humanitarianism is realized by such norms as being kind to others, not inflicting pain on anyone, sharing one's property or wealth with others, forgiving others who have harmed you, and respecting the worth of each person. Humanitarianism is supported by such beliefs as the brotherhood of all men, the expectation that kindness to others will be reciprocated or at least is ultimately rewarded, that through others one can realize a fuller life, and so on.

Not all norms and values are congruent with each other. For example, humanitarian motives may be in conflict with (a) patriotic ones, especially during wartime, (b) success-striving, as one elbows others aside, and (c) individual freedom which is not constrained by the rights of others. For most of us, however, some system of priority of values is worked out, defining the situation in which one value is considered above the others. Rules as well as values are usually conditional. It is wrong to kill, but it is all right to kill to defend your country, to save your own life, to protect your loved ones from physical harm, or to prevent a dangerous felony (Turner, 1954).

It is because people lack agreement concerning the appropriateness of certain norms and values in specific situations that the concept of reference group is significant. The wider the differences within a society with respect to values, norms, activities, and situations, the greater the relevance of reference groups in explaining the behavior of individuals. From the normative standpoint, the influence of reference groups is explained in terms of (1) the development of relatively consistent norms and values by groups, collectivities, and social categories, and (2) the individual's efforts (a) to organize and make consistent his own attitudes, values, and behavior, and (b) to relate himself to his social environment.

2-3   THE CONSISTENCY OF REFERENCE GROUPS' NORMS AND VALUES

The internal consistency of a reference group's norms and values is a function of (a) the mutual attraction of persons to each other upon the basis of similarity in values and norms, (b) the common or similar situations they face, (c) the similar experiences they have as they interact with each other and/or with outsiders, (d) the sharing of perspectives through the process of communication, and (e) the rewards which that sharing provide.

Mutual attraction. People tend to initiate social relations with others whose views are similar to their own (Secord and Backman) or to continue their relationships with others whose views are like their own, while discarding associates whose views differ from theirs (Newcomb, 1961). As a result, likeminded persons tend to interact more with one another than contraryminded persons with each other. The motive for beginning and for continuing a relationship with others whose views are like one's own is each person's need for consensual validation, i.e., the need to have their own ideas about themselves and about the nature of their environment affirmed by others (Alexander, 1964).

Common or similar situations. People who face similar situations are likely to have similar problems and similar needs which need defining in terms of norms. The situation may be similar because they face a similar or common physical environment or because their social environments are similar. It is easy enough to see that the members of a primitive group facing a precarious environment will become aware that they face the same problems. It is not so obvious, but it is equally true, that persons separated in space but belonging to the same social category (race, sex, age) may also come to recognize their common fate. Because they provide the same stimulus value to others in terms of some stereotype, they may be dealt with by others of their social category in a somewhat uniform fashion. Norms develop not only for status positions but also for social categories, as most Negroes of the South will testify.

The facing of common situations is found woven into several theories of delinquency. As background for this we may refer to a study by Havighurst et al. (1962, p. 24) which reported that in their community study practically all of the delinquent gang members

were school dropouts. In addition to academic retar-
dation and failure, these boys were not well adjusted
socially. At school they did not get along well with
peers, teachers, coaches, or teammates. The social
disability of delinquents is also reported by Short
and Strodtbeck (1965, p. 230-47). With this background material we can see some empirical basis behind Albert Cohen's (1955) *Delinquent Boys*, which
endeavored to explain the subculture of delinquency
in terms of the lower class boys' common problem of
dealing with the invidious judgments of them by middle class persons. Similarly, in *Delinquency and
Opportunity*, Cloward and Ohlin (1960) approached the
problem of the subculture of delinquency in terms of
differential access to the means of achieving success
by social class.

The meaning that one attaches to a given situation is a function of one's past history as well as
to the external situation. How one interprets, or
even recognizes, a problem depends upon the perspective provided him by some reference group orientation.
The boy who recognizes his social inadequacies, his
social inferiority, or his own unfair competitive
situation, is using the norms and values of some reference group in making that evaluation. The consistency of a reference group's norms and values is
increased when the individuals of the group apply
similar perspectives to common or identical situations.

Similar experiences and needs. Normative controls tend to develop in areas of human activity
where the members become dependent upon one another
or upon the group for the satisfaction of similar or
complementary needs (Secord and Backman, 1964, p.
336). If the need is to perform some task, then
rules will develop around the task. In the case of
professional thieves, for example, rules have developed which related to the honest dealings between
partners, the granting of moral support, defenses
against prosecution and confinement, and the like.
In other words, the rules tend to develop in the area
of the need and its satisfaction.

Sharing of perspectives. Individuals who constitute a group interact with one another. One of
the principal forms of this interaction is giving and
receiving communications which convey each person's
opinions, ideas, and values. Through the communicat-
ive process, both in the sending and receiving of
information, the opinions, norms, and values of each
person in the communication network are affected, and
tend to become more similar (Newcomb, 1956; Thibaut
and Kelley, 1961, p. 42). As consensus develops, a
social value known as sharing is developed. The
sharing of viewpoints is itself rewarding, and agreement is further facilitated (Thibaut and Kelley, 1961,
p. 253; Newcomb et al., 1965, p. 224).

Communication can be seen both as a cause and as
an effect of consensus (Homans, 1950, p. 126). In
general, people prefer to communicate with those
whose viewpoint they share (Thibaut and Kelley, 1961,
p. 73). It confirms their image of the world as they
view it. When, however, it is perceived that a member of the group is not conforming (an indication
that consensus in his case is lacking), communications with him from members of the group tend to increase in order to get him to conform. But if the
group perceives that there is little likelihood of
changing the nonconformer, their communications with
him decline. At last, when he is considered hopeless,
he is dropped out of the communication network and
out of the group (Berelson and Steiner, 1964; p. 347;
Newcomb et al., 1965, p. 202).

Consensus is important even in the slums. In a
study of the social order of a slum area in Chicago,
identified as the Addams area, Suttles (1968, p. 91-
92) found an interesting process known as "taking
one's troubles to the street." This is an area of
the city in which families live in such congestion
that within the home nobody has any privacy. Near
kin become privy to many secrets about their kin, including such serious disclosures as those of abortion,
incest, illegitimacy, adultery, narcotics use, etc.
One would think that each family would try to keep
its own skeletons to itself, and yet many of the fam-

ily secrets leak out to street acquaintances of family members. The purpose of these disclosures is to
use one's neighbors as a kind of ideal "jury of one's
peers."

> "Where husbands and wives, friends, lovers,
> or street groups have come to the 'end of
> their rope,' they may appeal to this form of
> arbitration. For the older Mexican and Ital-
> ian men, it is particularly humilitating to
> quarrel with a woman because men are supposed
> to give commands rather than submit to argu-
> ments. Thus a woman who has been pushed to
> extremities may try to retrieve her situation
> by airing her complaints before the neighbors.
> Such displays are a staple for discussion
> among street groups."

Out of these communications, no doubt, some consensus
arises, norms are developed, and greater consistency
achieved in the social definitions used by those of
the neighborhood.

The sharing of perspectives and the development
of consensus is essential to the survival of any
group or society. William Graham Sumner (1906, p. 5-
6), for example, pointed out the function of folkways
(norms) in adapting a society to its environment, and
the necessity of folkways being consistent with each
other to reduce internal friction and antagonisms.
Otherwise, through conflict with other groups or
through maladaptation to its physical environment,
the society would tend to be eliminated. Natural selection also operates on subgroups within a society.
Gangs which develop dissension may simply break up or
their weak defenses against the law enforcement agen-
cies may lead to their incarceration and separation.
In general, those groups which are best organized
survive and perpetuate their internal consistency.

*Collective and individual rewards for sharing
norms and values.* Group norms develop and are maintained because they are found to be rewarding (Secord
and Backman, 1964, p. 333).

First, norms may be considered as means by which desirable ends are attained, and therefore may come to be enjoyed along with the ends themselves through the process of association.

Second, because of the norm, each individual can know in advance what to expect of the other, and whether a social exchange is feasible or not (Secord and Backman, 1964, p. 596). He does not need to communicate in each instance to see if a social exchange is agreeable or not, and what the terms of the exchange should be (Thibaut and Kelley, 1961, p. 138-39).

Third, the cost of social exchange is usually high for those engaged in unequal social exchange. For example, parents have almost unlimited power over their child (at least while he is young), controlling the child's rewards (food, warmth, affection) and the child's costs (pain, deprivation, isolation, disapproval), with the child having little control over the costs or rewards of his parents except through his conformity or nonconformity to their demands. Through the establishment of norms which deal with parent-child responsibilities the child is rewarded by norms that place limits on the exercise of legitimate parental authority and that require the parents to look after the welfare of their child. Norms reward the parents by granting them social recognition for being good parents, and norms recognize the legitimate authority of the parents in requiring obedience and respect from their child. Without such norms the child would have such a debt of obligations to pay off to his parents for their care that he would never be able to live a life of his own, or to take on the responsibilities of parenthood himself.

Fourth, awareness of norms is rewarding in that the norms usually promote the desirable social relationships in which others gratify one's physical and emotional needs. Without the coordination of the group through adherence to social norms, many individual and group goals could not be attained (Newcomb, 1959, p. 280).

And last, group norms are rewarding in that they provide definitive guidelines for social acceptance. By following them one can be assured a desirable place in society.

2-4   THE INTERNAL CONSISTENCY OF THE INDIVIDUAL'S NORMS AND VALUES

In the preceding section the idea was developed that each reference group has a tendency to develop and maintain a somewhat consistent set of norms and values. Each individual also tends to develop somewhat consistent sets of norms and values in terms of which he views his environment and guides his behavior. Various explanations of the fact that the norms and actions of each person tend to be consistent include the fact that (a) the social environment is consistent, (b) he accepts the norms of his reference group, (c) he is trained to be consistent, (d) the discomfort of cognitive dissonance motivates it, and (e) his own conscience, exercising surveillance, requires him to act and think along the lines of his norms and values.

The social environment is consistent. It is assumed that the individual does not assimilate isolated random values, norms, and behavior patterns, but that he assimilates them by sets which have been developed by each of the groups or groupings with which he identifies. So long as he uses the perspective of one reference group, his norms, values, and behavior should be relatively consistent.

Another way to say that the values, norms, and behavior patterns to which one is exposed are consistent is to say that his role models are consistent. In dealing with this problem, Alex Inkeles observed that consistency of role models is related to social class.

"Whether the diversity of models in the middle class is greater or not, it seems clear that they are more nearly *consistent*, and in a

number of ways. Middle-class parents are more
likely to be consistent in the individual handling of the child over time; they are more
likely to be consistent with the other in standards they present to and uphold to the child,
and probably in their public behavior as well,
and they are more likely to represent and uphold principles and modes of acting which are
also stressed by the school and other community agents. This consistency should not only
make the impact of the models greater but
should also enable the young person to inte-
grate the models into one internal standard
without excessive conflct caused by too dissonant an internal dialogue" (Inkeles, 1968, p.
122).

He accepts the norms of his reference group. We
have already indicated that persons are more likely
to choose as reference groups those with attitudes
and values similar to their own. It is also true
that those who are already in a group, collectivity,
or social category have a tendency to match their attitudes and definitions of the situation with those
of their reference group. Some reasons for this are:
(1) They are more likely to have similar experiences
through such identification. (2) If they are in interaction with each other, the distinctive problems
they have as members of the reference group require
the development of special terms (argot, slang, tech-
nical terms) to define and color their experiences
(Bram, 1955, p. 44). (3) Interaction and communication in the process of realizing common or similar
goals tend to develop consensus within the group.
(4) Our agreement with others is rewarding to them,
and we tend to supply that reward in order to receive
similar rewards and to sustain the relationship,
through which our own needs are met, including (a)
support for our self-conception and (b) consensual
validation (Sullivan, 1953). The latter refers to
support from others in differentiating between fantasy and reality. It is an important requirement for
identity as a normal being. Autistic thinking, which
does not distinguish between reality and fantasy, re-

sults in penalties from nature and from one's fellows,
since the autistic individual is considered mentally
ill.   One's own definition of reality comes to him
largely from the society in which he is nurtured, and
on occasion a subcultural definition of reality may
be at variance with that of society at large.   The
"reeferhead," for example, may belong to a clique
which defines marijuana smoking as pleasant and desirable, while his opposite, the "square," defines the
man on pot as mentally ill.   Without his reference
group to define and describe marijuana smoking for
him, most persons exposed to the drug would consider
the experience both frightening and unpleasant (Becker, 1963, p. 41-58).

The norms of one's own group provide him with
his definition of the situation.   A rather strong
case for this was made in a study of homicide by Marvin Wolfgang (1958, p. 329).   He contended that in
some sectors of American society physical aggression
and violence are required rather than condemned in
certain situations.   In spite of laws which forbid it,
lower-class underprivileged people expect one another
to engage in violence when they feel threatened.   Under these circumstances, Wolfgang concluded,

> "The value system of the reference group
> with which the individual differentially asso-
> ciates or identifies determines whether as-
> saultive behavior is necessary, expected, or
> desirable in specific situations."

He is trained to be consistent.   Each individual
is required to act in predictable ways so that others
can better adjust to him.   Consistency of thought,
word, and deed by each person is enforced by sanctions which penalize erratic and impulsive behavior
and reward predictable behavior.   As an appropriate
example of this phenomenon, we may cite George Homans
(1950, p. 178):

> "If you are a gang member, you know that
> the gang will probably be hanging on the cor-
> ner at a certain time, and that if it is not

there, it must be at one of the few other
places. The established routine enables you
to find your friends, to act sensibly and co-
herently without wasting time, and this kind
of behavior is rewarding. Many wise men have
pointed out that people are lost without some
framework of expected behavior. But the need
for routine does not account for its appear-
ance.... The interesting point is that by acting on your expectations you, and others like
you, are helping to create the very thing you
all need. The fact is that if the gang turns
out to be where you expected it, and you join
it there, you have by your action helped to
create the routine on which your future expectations, and those of others, will be based."

In the example just cited the consistency of the
individual's behavior is directly related to the consistency of the group in following a routine. However, there are expected differences between the behavior of the gang leader and that of the followers.
That is why we call one a leader and the others followers. The teaching of roles to each new member of
a group is instruction in what behavior is consistent
in terms of that identity. For example, while doing
research with the Norton Street corner-boys, William
F. Whyte (1955, p. 304) learned that his role pre-
scription was not the same as the others:

"Trying to enter into the spirit of the
small talk, I cut loose with a string of ob-
scenities and profanity. The talk came to a
momentary halt as they all stopped to look at
me in surprise. Doc shook his head and said,
'Bill, you're not supposed to talk like that.
That doesn't sound like you.'"

William F. Whyte's experience in the slums of
Boston was not an isolated phenomenon. In a study of
a Chicago slum, Suttles (1968, p. 78, 92) found a
strong pressure on the slum dweller to be true to his
own identity:

"Street life in the Addams area carries with it a number of consequences. The homogeneity of its groupings and its informal setting encourages an exchange of intimacies that might otherwise be kept secret, or, at least withheld from explicit admission. Since the facts of one's private life inevitably contain an element of shame, they invariably expose one's failure to meet the ideal standards of public morality and taste. In most of the local street groupings those intimacies have been regularly and persistently exchanged to the point that practically no one can claim an unblemished social character. Since almost everyone has fallen so far from grace, there is little attempt to keep up pretensions or to appeal to public standards as an effective blueprint for action. In turn, having been party to so many little personal disclosures, each individual has implicitly acceded to the primacy of personal loyalties at the expense of public standards of behavior. Social sanctions, then, are exercised primarily when someone deviates from personal precedent rather than from public standards....

"... general morality is neither a dependable blueprint for action nor an appropriate way of treating people with whom the residents have shared so many intimacies. Where possible, then, each individual is evaluated against his own historical precedents. In turn, sanctions are exercised primarily when someone deviates from what others feel to be his 'true self'; it is then that people become 'phonies,' 'finks,' or 'jive.'"

We have already described the manner in which reference groups influence behavior by defining for the individual his self-identity and prescribing the appropriate roles for that identity. Here we have endeavored to add the observation that there are social pressures upon each to keep a given identity through time, with the consequence that behavior associated with that identity tends to become stabilized and consistent.

He endeavors to avoid cognitive dissonance.
There appears to be some individual variation in the
degree to which internal inconsistencies produce unpleasant feelings, but there seems to be a general
tendency for people to try to avoid inconsistency for
emotional reasons. The individual's efforts to make
his ideas consistent with each other and his behavior
consistent with his ideas was observed in the research of Leon Festinger (1957), and was explained by
the "cognitive dissonance" theory. By definition, a
cognitive element is any knowledge obtained or be-
lieved about his environment, his self, or about his
behavior. Dissonance is said to exist when there is
an inconsistency between two or more cognitive elements such that the acceptance of one implies the
obverse about another related cognitive element (Secord and Backman, 1964, p. 115). Cognitive dissonance is a matter of degree, and is thought of as the
weighted sum of the dissonant elements divided by the
weighted sum of the consonant elements, the weights
being determined by the relative importance of the
cognitive element in question. For example, a person
may enjoy smoking but receive information that it is
bad for his health. According to the cognitive dissonance theory, if both of these elements--the desire
to smoke and the desire to have good health--are
equally important, the person will be in an unpleasant state of uncertainty and tension, which provides
the motivation to change his behavior and/or his
ideas. He may change the environmental cognitive
element by shifting to filter tip cigarettes which
reduce the hazards to his health, or he may change
his reference groups such that he now has fuller support from his friends and associates to continue
smoking. A third solution is to change the ideas he
has about health and/or smoking (Secord and Backman,
1964, p. 117). Rephrasing this example in terms of
criminology, a person may want to steal but becomes
aware that if he continues to steal he will be caught
and sent to prison. The first solution is to stop
stealing and avoid the risk of prison. The second
solution is to reduce the risk of apprehension by
stealing only where the risks are low or by seeking
out friends and associates who support crime as a way

of life. The third solution is for him to convince himself that although there is a risk of going to prison, the rewards are worth it.

Although cognitive dissonance theory does not tell us how a person will endeavor to reduce his dissonance, and hence is lacking in predictive powers, it does provide us with some very helpful insights.

Cognitive dissonance theory may be stated in terms of exchange terminology (Thibaut and Kelley, 1961, p. 174; Brehm and Cohen, 1962, p. 39, 202-217). If a person experiences cognitive dissonance because he has accepted outcome A at the expense of outcome B, he can reduce the dissonance by re-evaluating outcome A upward and outcome B downward, increasing the difference between them.

In addition to making A or B outcomes seem more or less desirable, alteration of the subjective probability of attaining each is also pertinent to dissonance reduction. The research of Atkinson and Reitman (1958) shows that the motivation to achieve a goal is a function of (a) the desirability of the goal and (b) the expectancy of attaining it. Goals which are difficult to achieve offer more satisfaction but have less likelihood of success. For that reason, motives are strongest when the probability of success is 50-50. A person can reduce his motivational drive toward B by saying that the task is either too difficult to succeed or so simple the goal isn't worth the effort.

The cognitive dissonance theory should also be considered in relation to the degree of free choice the individual has in selecting or evaluating the situation (Secord and Backman, 1964, p. 148). The research of Brehm and Cohen (1962) shows that dissonance is unlikely to occur in a situation of forced compliance. This means that attitudes are little changed by offering excessive rewards for compliance or excessive penalties for noncompliance (Secord and Backman, 1964, p. 118). It means also that one way a person may avoid dissonance is to convince himself

that he really has no choice but to do as he did
(Secord and Backman, 1964, p. 157). He may do that
by assigning a relatively low subjective probability
of success to what would otherwise be considered acceptable solutions or alternatives. This means that
when underprivileged persons feel that law-abiding
behavior is unlikely to offer them the rewards they
desire and feel entitled to, they can engage in law-
violating behavior with less dissonance than if they
felt that the potential rewards of virtue offered
them a free choice.

Only those cognitive elements which are related
to each other in the mind of the individual can produce dissonance. They may be related to each other
(a) through the fact that the objects, properties, or
events fall into the same category, or (b) through
the perception that they are causally linked with
each other (Newcomb et al., 1965, p. 31 and 121).
Both (a) and (b) are largely determined by culture.

An important inference from cognitive dissonance
theory is that individuals tend to maintain stable
social relationships in order to avoid dissonance and
to validate their values and norms (Newcomb et al.,
1965, p. 146-48). Those people who have a low valua-
tion of themselves or who have repeatedly experienced
failure, frustration, and punishment tend to experience dissonance when they are praised or find success
and may therefore be inclined to seek out persons and
situations which give them the image of themselves or
of reality that they are used to (Brehm and Cohen,
1962, p. 178-80). Those who anticipate success and
have high self-regard feel less dissonance when their
social environment supports these goals. In either
case, to avoid dissonance an individual must not only
have internal consistency, but his norms and goals
must be consistent with those held by persons with
whom he interacts.

Cognitive dissonance theory can be tied in with
the observation that there is a positive correlation
between (a) the strength of the social tie of a person to a reference group and (b) the power of the

norms of that reference group to influence his behavior. We may assume either variable to be antecedent and hence causal. The breaking of a tie with another (whether due to circumstances, the behavior of ego or alter, a more powerful claim by an alternative reference group, or other factors) lessens the moral support given to the norms supported by alter. On the other hand, when ego is disillusioned and alienated from a normative system because (a) the normative system is dissonant, proclaiming an interest in peace but engaging in war, claiming equality while practicing segregation, etc., or (b) the normative system inhibits ego from taking what he considers to be a desirable course of action, then ego may endeavor to avoid all the alters who support the dissonant or inhibiting norms which cause ego to experience cognitive dissonance. Regardless of which comes first, the weakening of a social tie or the weakening of a social norm, there are numerous examples in the literature on deviant behavior to support the causal relation between the two. When an individual moves into a new social world there is general estrangement from the old. For example, John Clausen (1961) reported that before the drug addict began to use drugs he had already cut loose from conventional groups; McClosky and Dahlgren (1964, p. 213) determined that voters who became separated or alienated from their families were more likely to hold different political views than those who maintained family solidarity; Clinard and Quinney (1967, p. 250-51) inform us that the first stage of becoming a homosexual is to feel different from other boys and to be alienated from them; Becker (1963, p. 70) states that those who come to use marijuana sever most of their social contacts with nonusers; Greenwald (1958, p. 143) in a study of call-girls found that these girls had drifted to the big city after becoming alienated from others in their small town by their unconventional behavior, and were then free to form associations with others whose views were like their own; Lemert (1953) wrote that naive bad check writers had an inordinately high rate of alienation from their families; Haskell (1960) has pointed out that the attitudes (norms and values) a lower-class boy brings home with him may cause him to reject the goals and social norms of his parents, to downgrade his parents, and then to become alienated from them, with resulting lessening of cognitive dissonance. By changing reference groups (social ties + norms) the actor lessens the cognitive dissonance he would have felt had he engaged in behavior classified as deviant by his former associates or by their norms.

In an article on "Social Disintegration as a Requisite to Resocialization," Peter McHugh (1966) argued that continuing a relationship with another reinforces the values held by the other, and that old values can only be discontinued by discontinuing the relationship with the other. The problem posed by imprisonment is that one finds there his friends who continue to reinforce old values. To break up the old values, McHugh proposes proceeding along somewhat along the same lines that the Chinese did in brainwashing American prisoners of the Korean War. They broke up the prisoners' lives by normatively meaningless events, dislocating the ordinary sequence of activities; by socially isolating individuals from one another, they subverted interpersonal relationships which supported the old values. Such a procedure makes possible the establishment of new relationships with the custodial force which then provides the new values.

Cognitive dissonance theory is also relevant to the process of selective perception (Secord and Backman, 1964, p. 177), one's evaluating of new information in the light of information which the individual already has. This helps to protect him against accepting dissonant elements. Incoming information is also evaluated in terms of the credibility of the informant; this evaluation is largely in terms of the informant's expertness and trustworthiness (Kelman, 1961, p. 65; Newcomb et al., 1965, p. 100). That is, the informant should know the truth and be likely to tell the truth to the recipient who is evaluating it. This brings us back to reference groups, for they serve an important function of establishing guidelines for the credibility of an information source

(Secord and Backman, 1964, p. 210). The guidelines provide the individual with (a) criteria for judging information sources, e.g., that he is a member of the ingroup and was in a position to secure the information required, and (b) the names and identities of specific persons who are to be acceptable as reliable informants. In other words, to work effectively with delinquents and criminals (as well as with other deviants) one must first gain their confidence.

His conscience requires consistency. In their book, *New Light on Delinquency and Its Treatment*, William Healy and Augusta Bronner (1936, p. 10-12) described how conscience is developed in a child. Briefly, the child forms a positive emotional attachment to another person who supports a set of moral norms. The child's thoughts of wrongdoing are inhibited by the realization or the fear that violating the norm will upset or alter the desired social relation with the person who supports the norm. That other person, usually the parent, has become the child's reference group. If the child learns the norm, but has no desirable social relation with a person who supports the norm, the child can violate the norm without guilt. In this case, there is no reference group which incorporates the norm, so the norm has not been internalized by the child.

The Healy and Bronner study was a comparison of 105 delinquents with 105 controls, each of whom was a sibling of one of the delinquents. Thus delinquents and controls came from the same homes. The authors reported great differences in the parents' feelings and behavior toward the delinquent as against the nondelinquent sibling. This was especially documented in the case histories of eight pairs of twins, only one of whom was delinquent. Other indirect evidence was presented to show personality and treatment differences between delinquents and controls.

The inference from the results of the Healy and Bronner study is that frustrated, unhappy children had real or fancied feelings of parental rejection. Not having their emotional needs met at home, there

Table 1
Number of Delinquents and Controls Manifesting
Various Symptoms or Receiving a Given Treatment*

Symptoms & Treatments	Delinquents	Controls
Indicators of Maternal Rejection		
Much worry during pregnancy	10	3
Very sickly during pregnancy	13	6
Indicators of Unhappy Childhood		
Cross, fussy babyhood	14	5
Difficult toilet training	31	13
Indicates Spoiling		
Many or severe illnesses	28	8
Behavior Idiosyncracies	44	24

*Healy & Bronner, p. 74-75

was a tendency to satisfy them elsewhere, possibly through delinquent activities. Children who did not have strong emotional bonds with their parents not only were more inclined to seek substitute satisfactions, but were also less restrained by internalized parental norms.

In a thorough review of the literature on the incorporation of moral values in the child, Eleanor E. Maccoby (1968) considered two general views of moral development--the developmental and the social-learning views. The former is characterized by Jean Piaget in his *The Moral Judgment of the Child* (1948) and by Lawrence Kohlberg's *Stages in the Development of Moral Thought and Action* (1969). Both are concerned with the cognitive aspects of moral growth, the child's understanding of moral rules being related to the level attained by his thought processes.

Piaget sees the child as initially learning the rules laid down by authority, being initially unable to evaluate the other's conduct in terms of the other's intent because he still lacks the ability to place himself in the role of the other. In this first stage, behavior is seen by the child as categorically right or wrong, judged by the act rather than by the actor's intent. Only later when the child is socialized by his peers and develops the

capacity to empathize with others is he able to see
the need for mutual respect and reciprocity in the
application of rules. Instead of rules now being
categorically applied to all situations, each rule is
interpreted within a social context.

According to Maccoby (1968, p. 239):

"Kohlberg distinguishes different degrees
of internalization in the acquisition of moral
values. At the pre-moral level, standards of
judgment are external to the child, and the
motivation for conforming to the standards is
also external in the sense that the child is
governed by external rewards and punishments.
At Level 2, standards are still largely external, although the child can now be governed by
his own knowledge and anticipation of what his
parents consider right and wrong. The motivation to conform has become more internal, however. Although he feels he himself cannot
judge what is right and wrong, he feels an inner compulsion to conform to what his parents
have defined as right and wrong. Even if he
knows he could escape detection for wrongdoing
or may not get a reward for right-doing, he
still feels discomfort over deviance and pleas-
ure over conformity. At Level 2, he also feels
some obligation to enforce upon others the
rules which he has accepted from identified-
with authority figures. At Level 3, the standards as well as the motive to conform have become inner; they are felt as emanating from
the self, and no longer depend upon the support of external authority. They are the product of multiple role taking, with many models
other than the parents (Kohlberg here draws
upon Mead's concept of the generalized other).
At this stage, it is much more difficult to
get the child to change his standard upon the
basis of authoritative pronouncements. Kohlberg says that 'conscience' at this age means
'not only a painful feeling or a warning voice
associated with violating an external rule,

but an inner process of thought and judgment
concerning the right.' It is at this later
stage that moral judgment has become fully internalized and also rational. In one sense,
it is only at this stage that the individual
may be thought of as being truly 'moral' at
all."

The developmental view of moral norms implies
that conscience is a product of socialization, and
that its development proceeds faster for some individuals than for others.

The second general view of morality discussed by
Eleanor Maccoby (1968, p. 240-51) is that of social-
learning theory. Basically, it views the acquisition
of moral behavior like that of all other behavior,
through the process of learning by reinforcement
(positive and negative). In social-learning theory
the parents play a very significant role, since the
parents serve as the most consistently available reinforcers. Being ever present as models and as those
best in a position to reward or punish, their influence is great. It is recognized here that the parents who have the most influence in shaping the moral
development along socially desirable lines are those
who provide reinforcement for conformity to parental
norms by their warmth and affection.

With the research of Bandura and Walters (1963),
social-learning theory was enlarged to include the
observation that behavior can be acquired experimen-
tally through observing models, without direct reinforcement of the observer. Behavior is learned then
by either modeling, direct reinforcement, or both.
In this process, parents play a significant role as
models as well as reinforcers.

The classical study of Hartshorne and May (1928)
showed that moral judgments may be basically inconsistent. Honesty, e.g., is not a general trait, but
applies to the situation. The boy who will not steal
may cheat on an exam, and vice versa. The generaliz-
ing of moral behavior is related to the issue of con-

sistency, with which this chapter is concerned. How do learning theorists deal with it?

The generality of moral behavior is a function of the reinforcement contingencies in various situations, and the consistency of one's parents (and other significant persons) in the different areas of morality. Generality is assumed by learning theorists to exist to the degree that one's role models are consistent. It is seen as an end product. In contrast with this view, the developmental view of Piaget and Kohlberg is that generalization comes first, followed later by discrimination as to situation.

Whether we view "conscience" as based on affective experience (Healy and Bronner), a higher stage of cognitive development (Piaget and Kohlberg), or the end product of reinforcement (Bandura and Walters), the end result is pretty much the same. The behavior of the person tends to be guided by moral norms or principles, and to that degree tends to become consistent. It is then less dependent upon situational differences in the probability that behavior will be monitored. The actor in the final stage is his own ever present monitoring agent, carrying out sanctions (positive or negative) whenever needed upon himself (Thibaut and Kelley, 1961, p. 240-42).

2-5   SUMMARY

In the discussion of the status aspect of reference group behavior it was seen that reference groups affect behavior by training individuals to define themselves in relation to other people and the social structure, requiring that they follow the norms prescribed for persons with their identity, and enforcing their demands through sanctions. The reference group is attractive to the individual largely in terms of a satisfactory self-definition and in terms of the physical and moral support which the reference group provides.

The reference group, seen in its normative aspect, influences human behavior by molding each individual's set of norms and values into a consistent set, and prompting him to make his set consistent with that of those with whom he interacts or with whom he identifies. When his norms are not consistent, and he becomes aware of it, he is motivated to alter his norms, values, and/or behavior so that they become congruent.

3. WHAT DETERMINES THE CHOICE OF REFERENCE GROUP?

It is postulated that an important determinant of a person's behavior is his reference group, whose acceptance he desires and from whose perspective he defines his social situations. One's reference group is especially relevant in those situations in which a person is pulled in several different directions by various reference groups who define his situation differently. In such a situation a person may follow the pressure of one group to the exclusion of the others, try to reconcile several pressures by working out a compromise solution, or leave the conflicting demands behind him by seeking out a new reference group with which he feels more congenial. In each case the general problem raised is: what determines his choice of reference group?

There are numerous variables which must be accounted for in explaining a person's choice of reference group. For purposes of analysis they may be classified as (a) the social situation, (b) his own needs; (c) his normative orientation, and (d) the social demands. They are intercorrelated, as seen in the observations that the social situation is defined in terms of the person's needs, norms, and social pressures; that many of his needs are socially derived, developed through reinforcement in a social setting; and that the demands of one's fellows rest in large part upon a normative orientation which they share with the actor. However, each of these variables will be considered separately.

3-1   THE SOCIAL SITUATION

The social situation may be considered either as an independent or a dependent variable. Initially, it will be considered as independent, operating through the fact that it calls to the actor's mind (a) his relation to his reference group and/or (b) the normative content of his reference group. Since most responses are keyed to situations, the situation frequently resolves for a person that reference group which is most appropriate and the personal identity which he must assume.

First, he is only segmentally identified with most of his reference groups and their values, the situation telling him which reference group is appropriate (Turner, 1955, p. 131; Merton, 1957, p. 239 and 286). For example, officers and enlisted men fight shoulder to shoulder while in battle, but later when the crisis is over they tend to separate into two different distinct peer groups. Different reference groups are also relevant to different spheres of activity (Merton, 1957, p. 326). At work a man's reference group includes his superiors and his peers. His wife has no part there. In the evening when he goes home he becomes oriented to his wife and family. At the pool hall or the club his colleagues will have his attention. Not only is the physical setting important. The expertness or the competence of the other to deal with an immediate problem may be a deciding factor. A man looks to his doctor for advice and care when he is ill or injured, but if his case appears hopeless he may then turn to his priest.

Second, the element of *propinquity* may have an important bearing upon one's choice of reference group. Those who are physically close to each other in a community, factory, or prison have a greater opportunity to meet, interact, and develop attachments or antagonisms for each other. Exchange theory (Secord and Backman, 1964, p. 39) helps to explain attachments in terms of propinquity as follows: (1) Persons living, working, or playing close to one another find it easier to get together and once they

interact and find it rewarding they do not need to
travel so far to get together again. (2) Those physically close to each other are more likely to be similar economically and culturally, and, therefore, to
have more in common. (3) After they interact they
become more alike through communication. (4) Continued interaction increases the predictability of the
other's behavior, thereby reducing the costs and increasing the rewards. (5) It does not take so long
to get together.

It is the belief in the influence of propinquity
in breaking down barriers between the races that has
led civil rights groups to promote desegregation in
schools and neighborhoods. The study of Deutsch and
Collins (1951), for example, showed white housewives
who lived in integrated housing projects were less
prejudiced toward Negroes than those who lived in
segregated projects. In the formation of cliques,
one's attraction is usually limited to those he encounters. The cornerboys studied by William F. Whyte
(1955), for example, all came from the same neighborhood, and it was observed by Frederick Thrasher
(1926) in *The Gang* that many of the gangs were based
upon neighborhood identification. The importance of
propinquity upon friendship formation is further cor-
roborated by Festinger, Schachter, and Back (1950, p.
33-46) and by William H. Whyte, Jr. (1956, p. 330-61).

Propinquity combined with isolation is a powerful force intensifying socialization and identification. In his study of the Coast Guard Academy, for
example, Sanford Dornbusch (1955) found that the influence of other reference groups of the new cadets
was removed through the stripping process and the
isolation of the military camp. Combined with isolation was the sheer monopoly of time and the demands
to interact exclusively with the new group. This, in
turn, increased the dependency of each upon the others for the satisfaction of their needs, increasing
group cohesiveness and further strengthening common
group norms. This same process is described, though
in less detail, by Donald Clemmer (1940, p. 301), who
pointed out that the chance placing of a new prisoner

in the same cell with a hardened criminal was sometimes a significant factor in his prisonization.
Through prisonization, the assimilation of the culture of the prison, the inmates came to recognize the
prisoner group as their reference group.

It is recognized that sometimes one does not
freely choose whom he will interact with, as in the
case of one prisoner who must live with another at
the command of the prison administration. Even in
the factory or in a residential neighborhood one may
have little choice over his neighbors. It may be argued that the boy who lives in a delinquent neighborhood has little choice over his neighborhood and
hence over his choice of companions. The parents'
control over the behavior of their children is in
part related to parental choice of neighborhood. Realizing this, some parents have changed neighborhoods
in order to break down the undesirable attachments
which propinquity had made possible.

Third, the situation may contain physical objects which through association suggest one reference
group rather than another. The setting of the church,
with its stained-glass windows with religious pic-
tures, the altar, the organ music all suggest the use
of religious models as referents. The sharing of a
common garb (clerical or military) and the insignia
of office or rank suggest using those categorically
similar to oneself in these respects as referents.
And the distinctive dress of guards as against that
of inmates may suggest to the inmate that his reference group ought to be limited to those dressed as he
is.

Fourth, the situation may be seen in terms of
subjective probability. Briar and Piliavin (1965, p.
39) remind us that some boys who appear to be committed to law-abiding behavior (conformity) will never-
theless engage in delinquent acts when they think
they will not be discovered. Discovery would not
only entail possible punishment, but also threaten
their current and future statuses and activities.
The same observation may also be made for boys who

are not committed to law-abiding behavior. Delinquent and criminal behavior is most likely to be engaged in under those conditions that minimize apprehension and official action.

Turning now to the situation as a dependent variable, we may observe that frequently people seek out
settings with which they are familiar, where they can
satisfy their needs, and where they experience less
dissonance (Secord and Backman, 1964, p. 116). The
person who has decided to commit an illegal act will
very likely seek out situations where the pay-off is
high and the risk is low.

The situation which counts is not the objective
situation but the situation as experienced by the
individual. Each person will screen out some elements in the situation and pay particular attention
to those which provide him with present satisfactions
or give him clues which enable him to gain some control over his environment (Thibaut and Kelley, 1961,
p. 85). The situation will be defined in terms of
the individual's past experiences and his expectations or hopes for the future. Relevant to the situation will be his goals, his self-identity, his place
in the social structure, the norms and values he has
assimilated, and his evaluation of various alternatives which he considers open to him.

3-2   HIS NEEDS

Although they may be variously defined and classified, every general discussion of needs assumes
that the individual is motivated to satisfy his needs,
both native and acquired, and if the needs are not
satisfied in one social relation or social context,
he endeavors, insofar as he can, to satisfy them elsewhere. This is the approach of W. I. Thomas (1923,
p. 4-5) in *The Unadjusted Girl*, in which he classi-
fies needs as four wishes--security, new experience,
recognition, and response. In his analysis, W. I.
Thomas assumed that if the girl did not receive affection from her parents, she tended to turn to other

referents for the satisfaction of that need, possibly
to an individual who, in return for satisfying the
need, requested or required the girl to engage in immoral behavior.

It is a fundamental assumption of street-gang
work that delinquent boys can be redirected through
the satisfaction of their needs. Irving Spergel
(1966, p. 40-41), for example, describing street-gang
work as a profession, urges the worker to be aware of
the boy's needs:

"The worker centers his attention on the
individual delinquent's concept of himself,
and his personalized relationship with significant others, observing particularly how
the delinquent relates to acceptance or rejection, frustration or stress, security or
insecurity in his daily living....

"It is possible that the individual who has
derived little affection, security, or support
from an unstable family group may be seeking
substitute emotional satisfactions through
gang membership. The gang serves him both as
a source of substitute affection, security,
and support, and as a means of venting anger,
resentment, and hostility against the adult
world."

The satisfaction of the boy's needs provides the
street-gang worker with a means for altering his behavior, according to Spergel:

"An understanding relationship is a *sine
qua non* for interpersonal problem solving efforts. As the relationship is developed, the
youngster begins to trust, confide in, and
depend on the worker. In the process of this
ego-satisfying relationship, the delinquent
gains security, develops respect for himself,
and may begin to see himself and others in a
different light. He may identify with the
worker's values, accept his version of reality,

and even take on the worker's aspirations for
his present and future functioning."

Basically, he is saying that the street-gang worker
becomes the boy's reference individual, and thereby
influences his behavior.

In an empirical study of secondary reinforcement
and identification learning, A. Bandura et al. (1963)
established that adults who were positive reinforcers
(that is, who satisfied the subject's needs) were
more imitated than those who were not. They further
reported from Staats (1965) that a person's reinforc-
ing value is improved with responses that were smil-
ing, companionable, respectful, affectionate, and
sympathetic. In other words, behavior can be rein-
forced by the gratification of social needs.

The satisfaction of an individual's needs is
considered a reward, and the frustration of a need a
cost, which he experiences in every social relationship in varying degrees. According to Thibaut and
Kelley (1961, p. 21), two criteria are used by each
person in evaluating the rewards and costs from an
interaction. The first is called *comparison level*,
or CL, which is the standard against which a person
tells if he is receiving satisfaction from the relation or not. Costs and rewards are evaluated in
terms of what he feels he "deserves." His conception
of what he deserves is determined by (a) what he has
received in the past, and (b) what he thinks his comparison group is receiving. The second criterion,
comparison level for alternatives, or CL_{alt}, is the
standard a person uses to decide whether to leave the
relationship or not. This is informally defined as
the lowest level of outcome a person will accept in a
social relationship in the light of available opportunities. In interacting with another person some of
one's experiences are rewarding and some are not. In
judging the desirability or attractiveness of the
relationship as a whole a weighing of various outcomes is made, giving greater concern for those which
are salient, or particularly significant. In apply-
ing the CL_{alt} the weighted average of outcomes with

individual A is compared with those one might have with individual B, or C, or D. For example, a young man may be attracted to girl A because his outcome with her is above his CL, but if he finds that his outcome with girl B is better, girl A falls below his CL_{alt}, and he will leave her for girl B.

Attraction is directly related to CL and dependence is inversely related to CL_{alt}. One may be attracted to another without being dependent upon him, and one may be dependent upon another whom he dislikes. When a person's outcome falls below his CL, his dissatisfaction inclines him to break off his relation to the other, but he may not do so because he is dependent upon him.

Dependence

Although a classification of needs may include that of dependence, that is not our concern here. Rather we will look upon dependence as a condition which limits one's freedom to satisfy various needs. When one person is dependent upon another he is reluctant to explore alternative opportunities to form new relationships or to take advantage of them if they should be presented (Blau, 1964, p. 161). The origin of dependency may be due to either fate control, secondary reinforcement, and/or the removal of alternatives.

By *fate control* is meant that another can control one's outcome, making it better or worse, but there is little he can do to control the outcome of the other (Thibaut and Kelley, 1961, p. 102, 170). Under these circumstances, even though one's outcome is below what he would like it to be, the other is in a position to make it even worse if he should try to break off the relationship. A gang member, for example, may want to quit, but cannot do so for fear of being killed. In a situation of fate control the individual has learned that he can maximize his rewards by compliance to the other's wishes, and that resistance to the other's wishes results in a marked lowering of the reward-cost-outcome.

In an article on delinquency prevention through revitalizing parent-child relations, Ruth Teffertel-ler (1959) describes a project at the Henry Street Settlement in New York City. Various types of recreational activities: athletics, trips, camping, as well as a place to meet, were offered by the settlement house, but only to clubs. To form a club it was necessary to have parental endorsement. The parents of the children involved had a meeting at which they discussed the problem of discipline while the children were engaging in supervised recreation. The parental approval to form the club had mutually desirable consequences for the parents as well as for the settlement workers. The children realized their dependence upon their parents for the club, and so accorded them more authority at home; the settlement workers had more control because they were accorded the moral support of the parents.

In the development of dependency by *secondary reinforcement* a person comes to need the presence of others in order to achieve more complete satisfactions and to avoid anxiety (Secord and Backman, 1964, p. 555). Through association, others who have been present habitually when one's needs were satisfied become intrinsically rewarding themselves. The presence of the other is comforting even when he is not at the moment satisfying a need.

Dependence is also related to *absence of alternatives*. In a more restricted sense, we may say that dependence is found among people who have limited opportunity to achieve status and/or acquire material possessions. The theories of Cohen (1955) and Cloward and Ohlin (1960) tie opportunity limitations to anomie and delinquency. It is a generally accepted fact that opportunities in our society are unevenly distributed by social class, and it is assumed that by equalizing opportunities in our society we can reduce crime and delinquency. A more recent article by Kobrin et al. (1967, p. 116-18) more directly ties opportunity theory to reference groups and street gangs:

"Theories of reference group behavior suggest that the choice of a reference group is frequently determined by the presence of some common element of status, probably ascriptive status.... These considerations imply a need for fuller utilization of reference group theory as a means of unifying opportunity and status interpretations of delinquent subcultures. Status goals are, after all, largely determined by the kinds of reference groups to which an orientation is formed; adults as well as peers are included among the reference groups to which adolescents are oriented .... The location in specifiable segments of the social structure of any defined population is likely to determine the range of alternative reference groups to which access exists.

"As noted at the outset, opportunity theory makes the minimal assumption, with respect to the dynamics of status, that blocked aspirations tend to result in a shift of status goals. Further, such shifts are seen as essential in accounting for variations in delinquent subcultures. It is in this sense that opportunity theory also constitutes a status theory. The principal question posed by the data of the present investigation is whether the status goals ultimately fixed on by various segments of the lower-class male adolescent population may be accurately represented as the outcome of a series of aspirations successively blocked, relinquished, and substituted....

"The data of the study suggest that the ascriptive position of a person within the relatively narrow confines of a local social system operates from the beginning to limit and ultimately to fix the kinds of status goals entertained. The constraints of ascriptive position as a determinant of status goals may be conceptualized as originating in *types* of social resources differentially available at

> various points in a social system. Not the
> least of these resources are opportunities
> specifically to acquire the skills and exper-
> iences requisite to the achievement of status
> goals indigenous to any ascriptive position
> occupied."

The relatively limited choice of status goals by
lower-class boys inferred by Kobrin et al. is consistent with the social disability thesis of Short and
Strodtbeck (1965).

The limitation of a person's alternatives may be
the result of a voluntary or an unwitting act by a
person. Thus when a person gets married, signs a
contract, or allows his emotions to close his mind,
he is surrendering options or alternatives. Lefland
(1969, p. 50) refers to the process of "encapsulation," by which a person psychically isolates himself
from very genuine options by focusing his mind on
some threat or anxiety. This is the process that
Cressey (1953, p. 118) describes the embezzler as
using:

> "At the time of their peculation they did
> not look into the future to try to determine
> the ultimate consequences of their "borrowing"
> but instead merely thought that it would some-
> how be repaid."

Encapsulation in this case rendered the actor imper-
vious to possible future sanctions and punishments,
and made him vulnerable to the easy solution.

A person may become dependent involuntarily by
someone else foreclosing his options, as in the situation of imprisonment, dismissal from school, or
eviction from a home. In prison the inmate is not
given the options of where he will cell or when he
will get up in the morning. If he tries to escape,
fate control is exercised over him. The boy whose
thoughtless behavior caused him to be labeled delinquent will find his alternatives closed when his record prevents him from obtaining a job of trust. He

may find that good boys do not want to associate with him, restricting his friendship to other delinquents.

Those who have important satisfactions outside of a group become less dependent upon it (Thibaut and Kelley, 1961, p. 23; Burgess and Akers, 1966). This means that boys who are receiving satisfactions from their peers, say members of their gang, are less dependent upon their families and, therefore, more free to do as they please. It can also work the other way. In later adolescence when boys approach manhood opportunities for gainful employment and for marriage open up. If accepted, these opportunities lead to the formation of reference groups which lessen the youth's dependence upon the gang and promote behavior which is both adult and conventional (Sherif and Sherif, 1965, p. 282; Spergel, 1966, p. 8).

The above considerations of dependency bring out the fact that although there is a tendency to prefer reference groups which satisfy our needs and to avoid or to be alienated from reference groups which cause us distress, some persons are so dependent upon significant others that they cannot escape them or break off their relationship with them (Empey, 1967, p. 35). To effect a change of reference groups it may be necessary to break down or to destroy an offender's dependency upon his current reference group.

Some Further Restrictions on Satisfaction of Needs

Thibaut and Kelley (1961) do not believe that all human behavior is a consequence of trying to maximize the satisfaction of one's needs at minimum cost. Some responses are so dependably under the control of a stimulus that there is little reflective thought about consequences, as when a policeman or fireman reacts to an emergency. There is also the situation in which a person has not had an opportunity to learn the costs and rewards associated with various behavior alternatives. When the routine interactions in role behavior develop, the individual tends to engage in expected behavior without thought of the conse-

quences. In addition, since the CL is judged in
terms of *salient* outcomes, those which are important
to him, it is possible for a person to give so much
weight to a desired reward (such as marriage to a
beautiful girl) that his costs (loss of freedom, obligations, duties) seem insignificant at the time.
Similarly, a boy's association with a known delinquent may be considered so rewarding in terms of his
needs for recognition, status, and money, that the
cost of incarceration seems trivial, especially when
the subjective probability of incarceration is low.

So far our discussion has dealt with reference
groups with which one interacts. In the case of collectivities and social categories which serve as reference groups, identification tends to occur with
those who are either the givers or the receivers of
rewards one would like to have. Change of reference
groups here would be related not to one's own outcome, but to the perception of the outcomes others
are receiving.

Among a set of potential reference groups, a person may be thought of as selecting as his own those
which satisfy one or more of his personal needs, ig-
noring those which do not satisfy his needs, and re-
jecting those which frustrate the satisfaction of his
needs (Homans, 1950, p. 366; Newcomb, et al., 1965,
p. 395). A reference group is "potential" only if
the individual is aware of it, the rewards it offers
him, and in the case of groups and individuals with
which there an interest in establishing a personal
relationship, the subjective probability of attaining
this relationship is high enough to provide motivation for it (Thibaut and Kelley, 1961, p. 87; Secord
and Backman, 1964, p. 532). From the viewpoint of
the actor, needs are satisfied by rewards or rewards
are those events or objects which satisfy one or more
needs. The needs of the same individual vary with
time. There is the matter of marginal utility or
diminishing returns, in which the need, such as hun-
ger, declines as it is satiated. Most of one's needs
are not inborn, but are developed through secondary
reinforcement, from which it follows that since each

person's experiences are different, each has a unique set of needs. However, since life is experienced in a social setting which has common elements for all of us, there are commonalities of needs. A partial list of them includes the needs for affection, understanding, acceptance, recognition, and a sense of identity.

Affection

Every child needs love and affection to develop into a normal mature adult. Adults need it to maintain and sustain their mental health. Maccoby (1968, p. 248) tells us that:

> "High degrees of parental warmth have been found to be related to nondelinquency, to responsibility, and in some instances to indicators of 'guilt' or 'conscience.' In experimental situations where the amount of nurturance offered by an experimenter to a child subject is varied, it has been found that children will more often imitate a nurturant model than a non-nurturant one, a circumstance suggesting that one of the factors underlying the greater success of warm parents in inculcating moral norms is that their children are more likely to learn from them through modeling.... The child who feels strong positive attachment and little fear toward his parents will want to stay in their presence (and hence the opportunities for teaching and modeling will be increased) and will also be motivated to gain their approval and avoid their disapproval."

On the other hand, when affection is denied a child by his family, there appears to be a tendency for him to seek out others who will provide it. If the others who provide the satisfaction for the child's need for affection are delinquent or criminal, his dependency upon them for affection or response inclines him to accept their delinquent and criminal norms and behavior patterns.

In the writings of Clifford Shaw (1933) is to be found a statement of reference group theory (before it was known as such) and the function of needs in controlling behavior:

> "The delinquent's relationships with members of his gang often serve as the chief medium for the satisfaction of his desires for intimacy and companionship. These relationships are much more spontaneous and intimate than the formal contacts with teachers, probation officers, and even with members of the family group. In many cases the boy is much more confidential and has many more interests and sentiments in common with his companions than with his parents or other adults in the neighborhood. Consequently, the gang may exercise a control over the boy's conduct which is more effective than that of his parents and through its influence he may develop attitudes and forms of behavior which partially or completely isolate him from his family."

The strong need of delinquents for affection is frequently alluded to. Spergel (1966, p. 81) tells us that gang members constantly seek proof that someone cares for them, particularly an adult. Eva Rosenfeld (1959) states, "Characteristically, delinquents reject the possibility that anyone--and especially official representatives of the society at large--really cares for them." At the same time, it is undeniable that gang members make an outward show of toughness that denies their true inner feelings.

Understanding

Apparently there is a need for people who share common or similar problems to enter into repeated interaction with each other (Sherif and Sherif, 1964, p. 90). This is seen in the formation of professional societies which help members deal with the problems of unmitigated role-sets (Merton, 1957, p. 388). It is found in the adolescent whose age-mates appear

to him as more capable of understanding his problems
than adults, since his age-mates have the same problems (Sherif and Sherif, 1964, p. 50 and 164). In
the slum areas, where relative deprivation is most
keenly felt as the youths compare their lot with that
of the middle class and where the home is likely to
offer less comfort, understanding, and love, peer
groups are formed by those suffering the same deprivations. These groups offer the necessary sympathy and
understanding.

We have already observed in an earlier section
that it costs less or is easier to interact with persons who understand us and whom we understand, thereby helping us to conserve energy. In addition, we
experience less cognitive dissonance when we are with
and/or identify with those whose perspectives are
like our own.

Basically, I suppose, meaningful interaction
with another, without which there is no social bond,
requires that one shares with the other a common perspective of the world as one knows it, and the latter
is nourished most by the sharing of common recent
experiences. This is the problem of the exconvict as
he leaves the prison world: many of the social bonds
he used to have will have deteriorated during his
imprisonment. We see this in sharp focus in John Irwin's (1970, p. 131-34) account of the felon:

"The returning felon must find a group of
people with whom he shares a meaning world in
order to start enjoying life on the outside....
In order for this to occur there must be a
fairly recent extended experience with each
other or experiences within similar situations
with similar meanings. A common occurrence
which illustrates the importance of recent
shared experiences for meaningful interaction
is the chance meeting of two former friends.
After the first few exchanges of news there
invariably follows a difficult pause when both
parties suddenly realize that they have noth-
ing to talk about. The conversation lags; it

is useless to try to continue. So with difficulty they part, both feeling uncomfortable
and disappointed in their inability to gener-
ate some of their lost rapport. What has happened is that the old basis for their rapport,
the shared meaning world, has disappeared
through time.... In truth, although they were
friends, they are now strangers.

"Another parolee reported to me that even
though he was back among friends, back with
his family, around people he knew formerly or
with new friends, he felt lonely most of the
time. The prison experience is not only a gap
in time when the shared meanings with old
friends fade, but it is also a time when the
individual becomes immersed solidly in the
prison meaning world....

"Some parolees, usually those with fewer
inroads into the outside social worlds and
who, therefore, are experiencing this aspect
of reentry, as well as other aspects, more
intensely, solve the problem of their loneli-
ness by interacting primarily with other ex-
felons--often persons they knew in prison."

Acceptance

In addition to understanding as an important requirement for a reference group, there is the need
for others to accept and approve of us, or at least
hold out to us the expectation that acceptance will
come in due time. The Gluecks' study, *Unravelling
Juvenile Delinquency* (1950), showed that the nondelinquent child had more friendly relations with his
parents than did the delinquent, from which Daniel
Glaser (1956, p. 443) has made the inference that
warm relationships inside the family strengthen identification with it. The writings of Slavson (1954,
p. 242), Aichhorn (1935), and Redl and Wineman (1955)
imply or state that the child therapist must establish a warm, friendly, uncritical attitude toward the
delinquent so that the therapist will be accepted as

a reference individual whose values will then become part of the child's orientation.   In Healy and Bronner's *New Light on Delinquency and Its Treatment* (1936, p. 7-13) it is stated that a child must have a satisfactory emotional relationship with his parents before he will accept their standards as his own.

Acceptance of a person by an individual or an informal group means that he is permitted to enter into a closer and more intimate association with them.   He is given companionship and a sense of belonging (James Plant, 1937, p. 95-96).   This involves the development of mutual obligations and moral support.   Ideally, acceptance means that a person is chosen because of *who* he is rather than *what* he can do, i.e., his achievements.   He can make any claim upon the other without it being refused upon the basis of a greater claim to someone else or the demands of adhering to an overriding norm or rule.   Ideally, one stands by his friends no matter what they do or how badly they fail.   Acceptance by one's family means that they will shelter him and support him whatever crime he has committed or no matter how poorly he is doing in school or work.   Failure of a family to give a child the feeling that he has their fullest support may cause him to be dissatisfied with his relation with them and to turn to other reference groups which are more accepting and less demanding.

Peter Blau (1964, p. 35-36) makes a distinction between associations which are intrinsically rewarding and those which are extrinsically rewarding.   In the former one individual is attracted to another because the association with him is itself rewarding. In the latter the attraction is based upon whether the other can and is potentially willing to provide him with some benefit.   Acceptance relates to the gratification of knowing that the other is interested in him as a person, and, therefore, the relationship is not contingent upon his possible failure to provide some extrinsic benefit to the other.

One attraction of the delinquent to his delinquent gang is the fact that he is uncritically accepted by them at the same time that he is conditionally rejected by his family and conventional society for violation of legal norms. The family and society, of course, expect the boy to change his behavior to conform to their expectations, but he changes his reference group instead (Newcomb et al., 1965, p. 414). Acceptance by either the family or the gang is actually conditional upon conformity to the norms of the respective groups, but conformity to the delinquent norms is not considered coercive since the gang wants him to do what he wants to do anyway, and, therefore, involves little cost to himself.

Recognition

One not only needs acceptance by a group or person, but also needs to have a preferred position (recognition) (a) in his reference group and (b) in society at large. He is, therefore, concerned not only with his place in the membership group, but also with the place of his membership group in the society or community as a whole. Recognition brings with it the reward of deference from others (Thibaut and Kelley, 1961, p. 45). It may be based upon either ascription or achievement.

The desire to achieve recognition for oneself may lead one to work toward distant goals, selecting as reference groups and reference individuals those who can be instrumental in this achievement (Newcomb et al., 1965, p. 299). It may also cause one to choose as associates or role models those who have already achieved some measure of recognition and thereby to profit from the fact that others will perceive him as sharing that prestigeful position. This natural tendency of the lowly to choose as reference groups those with more prestige is documented in a study of 187 new immigrants to Israel by Dr. S. M. Eisenstadt (1954, p. 177). He found that 90 percent of the new immigrants chose as reference groups those considered as conferring status (prestige) upon them in the social structure. Contrarywise, persons with inferior status are shunned for fear of losing status.

In prison, for example, the author observed that most inmates did not want to associate with abnormal sex offenders because to do so would jeopardize their own status among the other prisoners.

Assuming that the prospective member is motivated to affiliate with a group, the newcomer will tend to assimilate and conform to the values of the most prestigeful stratum of that group (Merton, 1957, p. 254). His conformity assures his acceptance and his acceptance reinforces his tendency to further identification and conformity.

Self-Identity

Closely akin to the need for recognition is a person's need to establish and maintain a consistent self-identity. Many people are uncertain what attitude to take toward themselves and, therefore, turn to others to provide the evaluation and direction that they cannot give to themselves (Thibaut and Kelley, 1961, p. 43). Identity support for such a person may be provided by (a) his awareness of the opinions and judgments others express toward him and (b) the norms and values which he and they use in making such judgments. It is clear that both the status and normative aspects of reference groups are relevant to this discussion.

From the status standpoint, one of the most important needs of adolescent boys is role support as an adult male. One function of an adolescent peer group is to affirm to each of its members that he is an adult and possesses all of the adult attributes. Each member of the group provides satisfactions to the other by giving him respect and providing role support for the identity he is trying to establish (Newcomb et al., 1965, p. 301).

A person tends to choose as a reference group that group which will support the kind of identity he is trying to establish.

"... He selectively interacts with other persons, preferring those who treat him in a manner congruent with his self-conception, and avoiding those who do not. Similarly, he selectively evaluates others, depending upon their attitudes toward him. He does this by liking those who treat him in a congruent fashion and disliking those who do not" (Backman et al., 1963, p. 167).

The gang not only provides the boy with affection, understanding, and recognition, but a favorable self-identity as well. Whereas the family may not validate the boy's image of himself as an adult male, the gang does. In addition, the gang provides activity through which his identity is affirmed (Hall, 1966, p. 266).

Kvaraceus and Miller (1959, p. 72) explain *non-delinquency* among lower-class youngsters in terms of their "realistic desire for upward mobility." Their status aspirations have not only given them a new anticipatory social identity, but also some measure of identity support from their family, school teachers, and other representatives of conventional society.

A reference group also provides normative support for an identity (Thibaut and Kelley, 1961, p. 42). One's attitudes toward himself must not only be congruent with that of others. Self-attitudes should also be congruent with the values of others and himself (Newcomb et al., 1965, p. 139). His training and his need for consonance require it. Others must not only support him but the moral rightness of his choices as well (Albert Cohen, 1959, p. 468). To maintain a favorable and consistent self-identity he will tend to select as reference groups those who buttress his sense of worth *and* the value system in terms of which their support is justified (Blau, 1964, p. 113).

3-3   HIS NORMATIVE ORIENTATION

In the earlier section on the influence of the
normative aspect of reference groups upon behavior,
reference groups were described as influencing behavior by inculcating the individual with its set of
norms and values, and then training him to make his
behavior consistent with those norms and values. The
reference group in that analysis was largely considered as the independent variable. Here the individual is considered the independent variable, exercising
some selection over his choice of reference group in
terms of its norms and values.

A person may take on not only the values and
norms of those with whom he associates, but he may
tend to associate with those whose values he already
shares (Alexander, 1964). It may occur as an adjustment to the condemnation of one's own reference group.
A person may break with his condemners, shop around
for others who approve of his deviant behavior, and
create or join a new reference group which approves
of the behavior condemned by his first reference
group. Thus a homosexual may be drawn to other homo-
sexuals or to others who condone homosexuality (Albert Cohen, 1959, p. 470). It may also occur when a
person moves into a new neighborhood or changes his
social setting. He will tend to seek out those of
his own religious faith, educational background, and
political or social orientation (Festinger, 1954;
Hartley, 1960).

The attraction to each other of people with similar interests is found in the autobiography of Stanley (Clifford Shaw, 1930, p. 80), a jack-roller with
a long juvenile record. He tells of his attraction
to the Chicago area of homeless men (Madison and
State Streets):

"Men of all nationalities and races, from
the four corners of the earth, were there and
brushed shoulders with crooks and gunmen of
the underworld. They were attracted there,
as I was, by cheap movies, flophouses, cheap

hashhouses, and most of all, by the human der-
elicts that make Madison Street what it is."

Stanley was also repelled by an alien set of
standards. He had slept in vacant houses, in all-
night movie shows, in poolrooms, alleys, missions,
and flophouses, but found himself uncomfortable in
the home of a childless kindly couple who treated him
like a son and even talked of adopting him (Shaw,
1930, p. 87-88):

"The surroundings of my new home and neighborhood took my breath away. My first day at
the foster-home was like a sweet dream. The
new luxury seemed to dazzle and blind me. My
father rode with me to work every morning and
home in the evening. We had nice lunches together at noon. He talked nice to me, gave
me spending money and good clothes, but I
missed my old pals and the gay life we had
lived. Here I did not have any boy chums,
but had to spend my time playing the victrola.
My foster parents didn't have much life, but
spent their time reading and playing a tame
game of cards. They had lots of company of
snobbish people, and they looked down on me.
Even if they were nice, it was because of
pity and charity. There was something miss-
ing. Eating at the table I was ill at ease.
I couldn't do the things just right, and my
foster-mother looked at my blunders through
the corner of her eye. I compared everything
with my sister's common fare and poor surroundings, and finally longed to go back to
my friends and pals. Back home I wasn't
dressed up all the time, and could play and
romp and gamble and swear. But here I was
not free to move and talk as I was in the habit of doing before. Everything was different
--strange and stiff. I felt out of place--a
city waif dependent upon charity. I had been
in jail half a lifetime, but now I was suddenly placed in luxury after life in a dirty hov-
el. My adventurous spirit rebelled against
the dry life and it soon won out."

The reasons why people prefer reference groups which possess norms and values consistent with their own lie in the greater rewards of self-other congruence with respect to values and norms:

(1) One's own values are validated.
(2) Interaction is better coordinated and less costly.
(3) One can avoid the strain of interacting with those who condemn one's values and hence of one's self.
(4) He does not need to be so much on guard against offending others by disagreeing with them.
(5) Social acceptance depends upon it.

One thing that helps to stabilize current reference groups is the fact that it is these reference groups which establish one's frame of reference in terms of which he evaluates other reference groups and their norms. It is his own reference group which establishes the credibility and trustworthiness of information sources which might upset the status quo (Secord and Backman, 1964, p. 210).

Sometimes a person is placed in a situation where he must choose between (a) sustaining a social relationship with a person or group and (b) supporting the normative rules by insisting that they apply equally to all. He may have to recognize either institutional obligations of friendship (particularism) or institutional obligations to the larger society (universalism). An important consideration in such a situation is the legitimacy of the claim or the power of the claim on the one hand and the kind of sanctions which one can expect for noncompliance with the demand, on the other hand. Samuel A. Stouffer (1949), in a study of the problem, found that there are individual differences between persons in their sense of loyalty to friend or principle. Stouffer and Toby (1962) reported that the more intimate a person's relation with the other, the more leeway he would grant the other in the violation of a social norm. Some of the differences between persons may be simply

differences in normative indoctrination. Albert
Cohen and Harold Hodges (1963), for example, found in
a social class study of 2,600 male heads of families
in three counties near San Francisco that the lower-
class respondents stressed their obligations to, and
expectations from, their primary group (kin, neighbors, peer-group), whereas the middle-class respondents supported the universalistic ethic which places
principle above personal loyalty. The particular-
istic stress was also found in a study of a Chicago
slum area (Suttles, 1968, p. 79).

3-4 THE SOCIAL DEMANDS

The social situation is thought of as varying
through time. The social demands, as used here, are
the general pressures upon an individual to take one
perspective rather than another in terms of (a) his
association with a group, collectivity, or social
category, (b) his place in the social structure, (c)
the social distance involved, (d) nonmembership group
identifications, and (e) the group's attractiveness,
especially in terms of its goal realization and its
cohesiveness.

Membership in a Group, Collectivity, or Social Category

It is expected that a person will identify with
and be loyal to those of his own kind and to accept
their norms and values. Membership in a group, especially a primary group, leads to the presumption
that one wants to stay, to attain a favorable status,
and to abide by its norms. Those who conform to that
expectation pick their own group as their reference
group. It is also presumed that one will recognize
his obligation to those of his collectivity and to
those who share with him the same status category.

A person's identification with a group, collectivity, or social category, ascribed or achieved,
sets limits or opens up opportunities for identification with alternative reference groups. When a per-

son has been labeled an "ex-con" many doors are
closed to him even if he wished to open them. The
consequence is that he is unlikely to accept as reference groups those who have rejected him. On the
other hand, those belonging to the right categories
are given opportunities to develop associations which
may lead to the choice of new reference groups. In
this connection, it was found that exprisoners who
were released to the military service had a better
later civilian adjustment that those released directly to civilian life. One of the reasons for this
appears to be the fact that the exprisoner returned
as a "veteran" rather than as an "ex-con," and that
he had a more acceptable answer to give concerning
where he had been during the past few years.

Where there are conflicts in the claims of various reference groups for a given individual, his
various reference groups supply him with the answer
as to which reference group he should follow. They
may do this by establishing priorities among the potential reference groups, serving as referees when
they are not actual contestants in the reference
group struggle.

Each reference group with which a person is interacting urges him to seek the approval of certain
reference groups and to ignore or be hostile to other
reference groups (Sykes and Matza, 1957; Newcomb et
al., 1965, p. 445; Brittain, 1963). The child is
taught, for example, to respect his parents but to
ignore "bad boys," and other persons whose value systems and behavior are considered wrong (Turner, 1956,
p. 323). If he belongs to a gang, it will tell him
to listen to the gang and to ignore the opinions and
values of his parents, the police, and other out-
group persons who are defined as his enemies. The
hostility and isolation from these out-groups then
remove them as potential reference groups.

By birth and ascription a boy is placed in certain categories. His in-groups and out-groups will
be determined in many cases by his age, sex, race,
religion, and social class. It is expected that his

reference group will be principally chosen from those
defined as in-group persons. Formed by the attitudes
of those about him, the boy's self-conception will
operate selectively as he chooses appropriate social
categories as his reference groups. Certain others
will be rejected because an inferior or undesirable
self-image is associated with them.

In short, people tend to identify with and to
use as reference groups those they believe to be similar to themselves in terms of any variable which
their society considers socially significant.

Place in the Social Structure

Edwin H. Sutherland's differential association
theory stated that the influence of behavior patterns
upon one was related to the frequency, duration, intensity, and priority of the patterns. These descrip-
tive terms also apply to a person's associations with
people. It is here postulated that the more frequent
and the greater the duration of the socially required
contacts with another person or group in fulfilling
his social roles, other things being equal, the more
likely it is that he will use the other person or
group as his reference group. One reason the delinquent gang has such a hold over its members is the
fact that the gang so defines his gang roles and responsibilities that it monopolizes his time, giving
other people little time in which to exert their influence or to satisfy his needs. It is also true, no
doubt, that one prefers to spend more time with those
who are already one's reference group.

One's place in the social structure can be defined in terms of those with whom he reciprocates his
roles. Role requirements usually involve at least
some social interaction, through which there is an
opportunity to formulate some identifications with
the other. In addition to specifying with whom one
interacts, and what behavior is expected, social
roles define the appropriate social distance between
participants, which has a bearing upon the formation
of identifications.

Social Distance

Social contacts may be classified in terms of social distance into roughly three categories: primary, secondary, and tertiary. The relations between a man and his family, a boy and his gang, a person and his neighbor are illustrations of primary social contacts. They are intimate and they are usually face-to-face. By definition, secondary social contacts are casual, impersonal, and segmental. They are more appropriate in the relation of a store clerk to her customer, the policeman to the motorist, the judge to the defendant before him. When the social distance is so great that it is one of outright hostility, as in the social contact between a gang member and the police, the householder and the burglar who comes to steal, we may think of it as tertiary. The greater the social distance, the greater the status difference, usually, and vice versa (Newcomb et al., 1965, p. 340).

One is expected to have as a reference group those with whom he has primary social contacts and to refrain absolutely from having as reference groups those whose social distance is tertiary or hostile. In short, a person's membership and position in a group, collectivity, or social category defines his appropriate social distance to persons located elsewhere in the social structure. This is the intensity factor mentioned by Edwin H. Sutherland. It is assumed, in addition, that the more intimate the social relations, the more likely it is that ego will identify with alters and use them as reference groups.

Nonmembership Groups

A person need not be in direct social contact with a nonmembership group to use it as his reference group. He may have as his reference a group from which he hopes to gain acceptance and with which he may hope to eventually establish a primary social relation. It is assumed that reference groups not only tend to be those with which one *has* intimate social contacts, but also those with whom he *hopes* to

secure intimate social contacts. Hopes are usually
based on some element of truth or fact. One strong
incentive is the realization that others in the same
position one now occupies, but at an earlier date,
have gone on to achieve the cherished goal of acceptance. This establishes the empirical validity of a
status-sequence (Merton, 1957, p. 283-85). The latter are the stages or steps one normally takes in
moving from one status position to another, as from
fiance to husband, star athlete to professional athlete, army private to army sergeant. In the field of
crime the customary sequence is from truant to shop-
lifter to petty thief to auto thief or the sequence
of errand boy for a racketeer to numbers collector to
a subleader position in the rackets (Spergel, 1964,
p. 97-98). These latter status-sequences in certain
urban communities give boys a realistic basis for
selecting their role-models from among those ahead of
them in the same status-sequence.

Through membership in a delinquent gang a boy
may be able to prove to older and more sophisticated
criminals that he is ready to be one of them. He now
has a foot-hold in the underworld opportunity structure (Cloward and Ohlin, 1960, p. 144-60). His aspirations, formed by those around him, lead him to
take on the ideas and behavior patterns of his role-
models. He is undergoing anticipatory socialization,
or learning the role requirements of a group or status before he actually occupies the status in question. At the same time, an aspiring young crook
finds that his gang membership and his delinquent
behavior are limiting his membership in conventional
groups. Each choice of reference group opens up some
avenues and closes other avenues of membership identification.

3-5 GROUP ATTRACTIVENESS AND SOLIDARITY

It is postulated that in general a person will
tend to identify with and use the perspective of that
membership or nonmembership group which has the
strongest solidarity or cohesiveness. The attraction

to the group or gang is more than the sum of the at-
tractions to individual members, the group as a whole
having an influence by virtue of its togetherness.

Each social group is usually in competition or
conflict with other groups, not only as it strives to
achieve or attain its collective goals, but also as
it struggles for the loyalty and commitment of its
members (Sherif and Sherif, 1964, p. 241). The
gang's conflict with outside groups--parents, teachers, police, rival gangs, and the community at large
--tend to produce solidarity by (a) pointing out the
need for loyalty, (b) increasing activity and involve-
ment (Jansyn, 1966), and (c) alienating the gang's
members from otherwise available reference groups.

Group solidarity or cohesiveness may be thought
of as either an independent or as a dependent variable. As an independent variable it is seen to increase the likelihood of the acceptance of the
group's norms. For example, Schachter (1951, p. 190)
cites Festinger, Schachter, and Back (1951):

> "There was a high positive correlation be-
> tween the cohesiveness of the social group
> (measured by per cent of a group sociometric
> choices) and the strength of the group stand-
> ard (measured by per cent of those of con-
> formers to the standard)."

It has also been pointed out by Donald Cressey (1955,
p. 118) that the readiness of members to influence
others to conform to group norms was related to the
cohesiveness of the group. Cohesiveness was instrumental in promoting intragroup trust and commitment
as well.

Turning now to a consideration of cohesiveness
as a dependent variable, we may begin by recalling
our discussion of the normative aspect of reference
groups. The consistency of reference groups' norms
and values (see Chapter 2) were considered as functions of (a) the mutual attraction of each person to
the group upon the basis of similar norms; (b) the

common or similar situations they faced, (c) the
similar experiences they had as they interacted with
each other, (d) the sharing of perspectives through
the process of communication, and (e) the rewards
which that sharing provided. Since the sharing of a
common set of norms and values (the normative aspect)
was important to the solidarity of the group (status
aspect) and these two are separate only analytically,
the above topics which relate to the consistency of
the group norms are relevant to our discussion of
group solidarity.

Attraction to Others with Similar Norms and Values

The solidarity of a gang is greatly improved by
its requirement that new members already accept many
of its norms and values through (a) participation in
delinquent activities with others prior to their admission to membership, (b) anticipatory socialization,
and (c) their acceptance of the moral rightness of
the gang's activities.

Facing a Common Situation

It has been observed that the members of each
gang are invariably drawn from the same neighborhood.
They are about the same age, and are frequently,
though not necessarily, of the same race and ethnic
background. Sometimes there is an additional tie of
kinship. This homogeneity of social categories to
which they belong enables them better to identify
with and to be attracted to one another.

The importance of one's attributes is increased
in the gangs that find themselves at conflict with
gangs possessing different attributes than themselves.
The conflict is then seen as more than gang against
gang. It is black against white, Puerto Rican
against Italian, or Irish against German.

The common situations they face may include dealing with rival gangs that wish to invade their area,

failing at school, handling authority figures (police, teachers, probation officers, parents), finding something to kill time, making a play for the girls, handling a personal inadequacy or stigma, committing a burglary or other theft, disposing of the loot, and/or avoiding arrest. We tend to identify with those who are "in the same boat" as we are.

Having Similar Experiences

Conflict of one gang with another involves both common and similar experiences. It is common in that it is shared, and similar in that the experiences are alike. Conflict with an outside group tends to produce solidarity within each so long as there is some expectation of success. The outside group may be another gang, the police, the neighbors, or even one's parents. The outside threat produces solidarity by its focus upon the collectivity and by the urgency of the individual's need to make a commitment to it. Each feels that unless he supports his group in this crisis, it will be destroyed or subjugated. The conflict increases solidarity also by the sudden elimination of internal dissention on items that now seem trivial. The reminiscence after the fighting is over helps each to collect some reward for his contribution to it. Read, for example, the following account from Short and Strodtbeck (1965, p. 201-202):

"This was a minor skirmish between two groups who had been feuding for some months. In the conversation with the director of the research program at the University of Chicago, the worker continued his report, describing the behavior of the boys after the skirmish, when they were in his car:

"In the car, Commando and the other boys were extremely elated. There were expressions like: 'Baby, did you see the way I swung on that kid'; 'did you see them take off when I leveled my gun on them'; 'you were great, Baby. And did you see the way I ...,' etc. It was just like we used to feel when

> we go back from a patrol where everything
> went just right (the worker had been a para-
> trooper in the Korean conflict). The tension
> was relieved, we had performed well and could
> be proud."

The amount of conflict engaged in by gangs var-
ies considerably. Those whose principal reason for
existence is conflict appear to have high solidarity
only while there is a fight in progress. At other
times their membership and solidarity decline considerably (Yablonsky, 1962). On the other hand, some
gangs are able to maintain relatively high solidarity
with relatively little gang fighting (Spergel, 1964),
e.g., the racket-oriented gangs of "Racketville."

The solidarity of gangs is strengthened by many
activities in addition to fighting. They engage in
"hanging," pitching pennies, card-playing, drinking,
bowling, baseball, horse-play, "signifying," joy-
riding in a car, attending dances, camping, excur-
sions, stealing, and even doing time together. These
experiences do not need to be delinquent in order to
contribute to the solidarity of the gang (Suttles,
1968, p. 182-91).

The gang which spends most of its time together
will be having many similar experiences. If these
experiences are pleasurable, the members will receive
secondary reinforcement, so that group satisfactions
later come from just being together. This promotes
dependency, the withdrawal of alternatives, and
heightened solidarity.

Sharing Communications

In addition to monopolizing time, the gang may
monopolize the interests of its members. For example,
the gang may become concerned about the social contacts a gang member makes with a stranger in the
neighborhood, the girlfriends a gang member chooses,
the clothing each boy wears, the way he cuts his hair,
his use or nonuse of alcohol and drugs. The expres-

sion of this concern for each member's activities has
the secondary effect of increasing the communication
flow between gang members, which in turn increases
solidarity by developing a shared set of norms, which
stabilizes their social relations with each other
into an integrated structure in terms of which each
person can develop commitments and trust in his relationships.

Advantageous to the development of solidarity
are verbal expressions concerning the benefits of the
group--its worthwhile *goals*, its use of pleasurable
and appropriate *means* to achieve those goals, and the
satisfaction of individual and group *needs*. It is
somewhat difficult to differentiate between means,
ends, and needs in a specific case because means
themselves are frequently intrinsic values providing
their own satisfactions. For example, some boys
steal an auto which they drive around the neighborhood to show off. Is the goal of the theft the pos-
session of the car, the experience of risk-taking,
doing something with one's pals, or the recognition
of others outside the group? It may be all of them.
The goal may be different for one of the participants
than for another; the goal may be complex rather than
simple. Theft may have a special appeal because it
gives a boy a chance to gain recognition, to symbol-
ize the throwing off of restraints, to attack those
who are economically better off than he or because it
is simple and requires very little in the way of effort. Regardless of whether the acts of the group
are criminal or noncriminal, whether they satisfy
needs, attain goals, or utilize desired means, the
solidarity of the group is enhanced by communications
within the group that it is worth belonging to.

In summary, taking Durkheim's distinction between mechanical and organic solidarity, we find that
solidarity is based upon (1) homogeneity of individuals with respect to mental and moral attitudes or the
sharing of consensus, a normative integration, and
(2) a heterogeneity of persons bound together in a
division of labor so that they need the cooperation
of one another, a status integration. In short, sol-

idarity is created by the development of consensus
and interdependence.

3-6   SUMMARY

The theory of differential association dealt
primarily with the influence upon behavior of the
differential behavior patterns with which a person
comes into contact. This theory, although true, is
seen here as a special case of the more general the-
oretical framework of reference group theory. One's
reference group--that "group" in which one wants to
be counted as an individual and whose standards and
goals he accepts as his own--affects his behavior by
(1) defining for him who he is, the roles and norms
which are appropriate for him to use, the values he
should support, and imposing sanctions for conformity
or deviation from the behavior or attitudes which are
expected of him, and (2) promoting the individual's
need to make his values, norms, and behavior inter-
nally consistent, and to make his values and norms
consistent with that of his reference group. His
choice of a reference group is a function of the social situation, the needs of the individual (and
their satisfaction), his normative orientation, and
the external demands made upon him.

4. CHANGING REFERENCE GROUP IDENTIFICATION

Because one's behavior (overt and covert) is assumed to be principally a function of the reference group he is using at the moment, control over his behavior is exercised by (a) affecting his choice of reference group and/or (b) changing the normative content of the reference groups with which he is now identified (Cartwright, 1951). Although not so labeled, the reference group approach has already been used in a number of delinquency prevention and delinquency treatment projects. The Boston Delinquency Project's operating philosophy was described by its director, Walter B. Miller (1959) as endeavoring to change the normative content of gangs through the use of street gang workers:

> "The theoretical concepts of the Boston Project's corner-group work may be summarized in highly condensed form as follows. During the age period from 12 to 19, the dominant set of influences on the behavior of members of lower-class adolescent groups derive from the group's conception of prestige-conferring behavior and valued objectives. At this age, intrafamily relations and standards of behavior set by parents have relatively little direct influence on the adolescent's day-to-day behavior. These factors, however, may have played a role in his becoming a corner-group member.

"On the basis of this concept, the Project took as its principal target of change the value system of the group itself. The primary device for altering collective values consisted of the introduction or facilitation of changes in the form of group organization. Such changes in form--generally involving the restructuring of the corner group into formally organized clubs--are initially perceived by group members in terms of simple facilitation of immediately desired ends: getting club jackets with money raised by putting on a dance.... Effective co-ordination of joint enterprises requires the imposition of internal sanctions on 'disruptive' behavior, and organized groups must maintain a 'rep' for law-abiding behavior to facilitate necessary interaction with the law-abiding community groups."

The Provo Experiment in delinquency rehabilitation by Empey and Rabow (1961) utilized the delinquents themselves as the reference group which instituted change:

"Whether they are members of a tight knit gang or of the amorphous structure of the 'parent' delinquent subculture, habitual delinquents tend to look affectively both to their peers and to the norms of their system for meaning and orientation."

They are not using the term "reference group" here, but it fits in with our conception of such groups being peers + norms. Now to continue this citation:

"Thus, although a 'bad' home may have been instrumental at some early phase in the genesis of the boy's delinquency, it must be recognized that it is now other delinquent boys, not his parents, who are current sources of support and identification. Any attempts to change him, therefore, would have to view him

as more than an unstable isolate without a
meaningful reference group. And, instead of
concentrating on changing his parental relationships, they would have to recognize the
intrinsic nature of his membership in the delinquent system and direct treatment to him
as a part of that system....

"A treatment system will be most effective
if the delinquent peer group is used as the
means of perpetuating the norms and imposing
the sanctions of the system. The peer group
should be seen by delinquents as the primary
source of help and support."

In the Provo Experiment the boys lived at home,
but came six days a week to the project center at
Pinehills. Guided group interaction was used. For
the most part, the boys made the rules and the deci-
sions on their enforcement. Each boy was induced to
show his sincerity by endeavoring to help others with
their problems. In a similar type of treatment institution in Essexfield, the development of a new argot
favoring reformation aided the boys to accept treatment and to help others in understanding their problems (Stephenson and Scarpitti, 1968).

4-1   THE STATUS ASPECT OF REFERENCE GROUPS

From the standpoint of status or his relationship to other persons, we may view a person's behavior as subject to control by affecting his choice of
reference group through (a) designating the social
situation which is appropriate for it, (b) defining
for him his identity, (c) making him dependent upon
his referent by the satisfaction of his needs, and
(d) improving the solidarity of his appropriate reference group.

Designating the Social Situation

In our discussion of the social situation (Chapter 3) we saw that the physical setting in which a

person was located (church, school, gym, clubhouse,
or home) gave him a clue as to which reference group
was appropriate. If certain physical environments
strongly suggest the selection of the wrong reference
group, one strategy is to move the individual and/or
the group to a different setting. The use of church
gyms would be superior to an athletic field in a vacant lot, if the latter had been used for immoral or
illegal purposes. The YMCA might be better than the
school gym.

The wearing of a boy scout uniform may make a
boy think and act like a scout, especially if being a
scout is important to him. Perhaps some kind of gar-
ment might regularly be used for doing good or char-
itable acts to build up the correct association and
then its use extended over a longer time period.

To some extent, the situation defines the identity of the other person as well as one's self.
Street-club workers may gain acceptance in a delinquent area simply by hanging around a candy store
which had previously been accorded the character of a
place that is safe, neutral, or friendly (Crawford et
al., p. 343):

"I spend many hours in the boys' hangout,
a candy store. I played the juke box, drank
coffee, did a lot of listening, and occasion-
ally chimed in on the boys' discussions. On
four occasions I asked the fellows to help me
choose some decent numbers. After that, they
changed the numbers I punched to play records
of their own choice. They don't do this se-
cretly, but openly and with good humor. When
they enter the store and I am there, they
greet me along with anyone else in the store
whom they know. And on the several occasions
that I have entered the store to find them
there, they continued talking or doing whatever they were engaged in."

Defining His Identity

In the discussion to follow, those reference groups whose norms and values we wish to promote will be labeled "X," and those we wish to weaken will be called "Y." Our strategy here will be to give the youth whom we wish to influence a self-identity which is consistent with group X and inconsistent with group Y.

If the training of a youth had been proper he would have the right reference group and there would be no reason to change it. He would then conceive of himself as a kind of person for whom criminal activity is forbidden. No person's identity, however, is permanent. It inevitably changes with his age and growing or changing aspirations, statuses, and social relationships. Through these changes Group X should support those identities which are either intrinsically good or which are intrinsically neutral but which are considered rewarding identities to the individual. It will find those identities which the target individual is trying to establish, e.g., adult male, and promote that identity in a context of law-abiding activities.

Desirable identities may be built or encouraged by a number of devices, which include the following:

1. Make it rewarding for the delinquent or criminal to take on the identity of one who is reformed by (a) making visible the rewards which the reformed receive and (b) granting him the identity of one who is reformed early enough that anticipatory socialization will have its desired effect.
2. Give the youth a status identity which requires lawful behavior, e.g., a position of trust, and then support his efforts to carry out the required roles by showing faith and trust in him.
3. Validate the fact that certain nonmembership groups are realistic aspirations for him. If he is lacking in the skills and training

which are required, such training should be
provided. This, I think, is what the Newgate
Project is endeavoring to do.
4. Strengthen his aspirations to "make it" as a
   noncriminal. Partly, this is achieved in the
   case of the prison inmate when he sees that
   others like himself have been able to stay
   out of prison after their release.
5. Explore with the offender the various identities he is interested in, the priorities of
   each identity, and the incompatibility of the
   deviant identities with his primary identity
   goal.

Development of Dependence

In our earlier discussion of dependency (Chapter
3) we saw that dependency was a function of fate control, secondary reinforcement, and removal of alternatives. We will relate each separately to the changing of behavior.

Fate control. It is not expected that reference
groups can be changed directly through the exercise
of fate control. To be effective in changing attitudes and behavior, fate control must be combined
with other methods. For example, fate control can be
used to remove a boy from the influence of his gang
by moving his family to a different part of the city,
drafting him into the army or some public service
unit, or even sending him away to school, but in the
new setting the boy must be attracted to desirable
role models before his attitudes and behavior can be
effectively changed. The weakness of the peniten-
tiary system today is the general failure of prisons
to substitute a better role model for the old ones.

On occasion, a boy will want to be law-abiding,
but the power of the gang is too great. In such a
case, the strong support of a street-gang worker may
allow the boy to make the claim that he'd like to go
with the gang, but the man wouldn't let him.

Secondary reinforcement by satisfying needs.
Basically, developing dependence by secondary reinforcement involves the establishment of rapport with
another by the satisfaction of his physical, emotional, and social needs. The strategy of the successful
street-gang worker is to satisfy the legitimate needs
of the boys with whom he wishes to work. At first
the gang members will be suspicious, and maybe even
hostile, according to Spergel (1966, p. 71-92) in
Street Gang Work: Theory and Practice, and they will
test him out to see if he is trustworthy. This test
is met in several ways, but first of all, the worker
is advised to demonstrate his acceptance of, and respect for, the youngsters. He must be patient and
friendly, tolerant of their verbal attacks on him,
and express a willingness to help them in various
ways. Since street-gang workers are generally as-
signed to the worst neighborhoods, many of the boys
have strong feelings of deprivation.

> "Gang members constantly seek proof that
> someone, particularly an adult, cares for
> them. They expect to be and seek to prove
> that they are unloved, neglected, and de-
> prived, at the same time that they want evi-
> dence to show their concerns and fears are
> unfounded. The worker must continually as-
> sure and reassure them that matters are not
> so bleak and terrible as they think. By his
> steady, unfailing interest and concern he
> must demonstrate that there are adults, of
> whom he is one, who care" (Spergel, 1966, p.
> 81).

It is only after a strong emotional bond between
the street-gang worker and the gang has been built up,
and after the thought of losing him becomes intoler-
able, that the street-gang worker is in a position to
set standards of behavior that are like those in conventional society. As the social bond grows stronger,
the standards of conduct can be set higher.

Spergel tells us (1966, p. 84):

"The worker who is warm and friendly, who
has gained the respect and admiration of group
members, may be used as a role model.... This
process of incorporation may occur without
conscious awareness on their part. It is the
result of the worker's appropriate way of meeting the members' needs for affection, guidance,
and productive activity. Thus changes in certain patterns of behavior occur in a generalized, nonplanned way, because of the worker's
positive relationship with the members. In
other words, the relationship *per se* becomes a
powerful dynamic for change in group goals,
norms, and values."

Peter McHugh's (1966) suggestion concerning social disintegration as a requisite to resocialization
is also related to the breaking down of dependence,
and so is relevant here. He suggests subverting interpersonal relationships through breaking up the
reciprocity of roles. Since complementary roles develop in a condition of propinquity, he would have
inmates in prison change cell assignments frequently.
Work assignments would also change frequently, so
that the prisoners would be continually in the company of strangers. Men would not be kept together
long enough for their initial suspicion of one another to break down. Tasks would never be allowed to be
carried to their completion, so that men would not
get the satisfaction of completing a task together.
The breaking up of ordinary routine events into ran-
domly occurring events, thereby making social activity unpredictable, would tend to make the prisoner
feel helpless and powerless. Although McHugh does
not carry the treatment process another step forward
with the building up of a new person, his suggestions
are very provocative, offering a new way out of an
old problem.

Removal of alternatives. An individual may be
dependent upon a reference group because he sees no
reasonable alternative to it for the satisfaction of
his needs (see Chapter 3). A person may be freed
from dependence upon reference group Y and made more

amenable to the influence of reference group X by (a) reducing the alternatives offered by Y and (b) enlarging those of X.

The slum area has been described as a place where there is a ready outlet for stolen merchandise. The fence operating a pawnshop, second-hand store, junkyard, repair shop, or other retail business, gives the delinquent ample options for disposal of stolen merchandise, as do the residents of the neighborhood who ask no questions. Closing these outlets has for years been a part of crime prevention programs.

Recreation and training programs also help reduce delinquent alternatives with a gain in conventional alternatives. Redirecting the use of leisure time, presently monopolized by the gang, is currently urged by recreation leaders as an aid in preventing delinquency. One of the big problems here is to reach the boys who most need such a program. The impact of recreation programs upon career options is especially salient when natural athletes are discovered, leading to athletic fame in collegiate and professional sports. The acquisition of skills and knowledge in areas other than athletics also impinge on leisure time otherwise free for gang activities, and have the additional benefit of opening up new options for employment.

Those boys who are dependent upon the gang because there are no real alternatives, so far as they can see, may be released from this bondage by opening up for them opportunities of which they had been unaware, or which they had considered beyond their reach. In the report on the *Provo Experiment* by Empey and Rabow (1961), it was argued that the treatment of these boys on an out-patient basis allowed them actually to compare the alternatives of legal and illegal activities in a community setting. They were given employment by the city and county parks, streets, and recreation departments. They could experience first hand the advantages of gainful employment over illegal activities, the latter carrying

a high risk of imprisonment and the former offering
social acceptance.

Solidarity

In an article on "Achieving Change in People:
Applications of Group Dynamics Theory," Cartwright
(1951) proposed that if a group is used effectively
to change people, the changers and the target people
should have a strong sense of belonging to the same
group. This means that the group should have cohesion or solidarity, promoted by such things as (a)
the individuals of the group liking one another, (b)
feeling that the group's goals are important, and (c)
receiving prestige from their membership in it. In
an effort to apply the Cartwright article to the differential association theory, Donald R. Cressey
(1955) stated five principles, the third of which is
relevant here:

> "The more cohesive the group, the greater
> the member's readiness to influence others
> and the more relevant the problem of conform-
> ity to group norms. The criminals who are to
> be reformed and the persons expected to ef-
> fect the change must, then, have a strong
> sense of belonging to one group; between them
> there must be a genuine 'we' feeling. The
> reformers, consequently, should not be iden-
> tifiable as correctional workers, probation
> or parole officers, or social workers."

In our discussion of this topic (see Chapter 3)
we related solidarity to the individual members' pri-
or acceptance of the group norms and values, facing a
common situation, having similar experiences (including that of conflict with an outside group), and to
the sharing of their experiences and ideas through
free communication. The application of these observations to the changing of group identification may
involve getting across the idea that many of the
norms of conventional groups are similar to those of
delinquent groups, e.g., loyalty is a noble quality;
it may also involve putting the change people and the

target people into the same situation (going on an
outing, cleaning up the neighborhood, correcting some
neighborhood abuse, etc.); joining together to break
down a social barrier (race, criminal status, poverty,
etc.); and the free communication of change and target people. It would appear that this has been
achieved most successfully by the street-gang workers.
The solidarity of the group as well as the dependence
of the boys upon their street-gang worker is a concern of street-gang workers. When the activities of
the gang can be redirected along socially desired
ends, it is desirable to increase group solidarity.
When it appears that the gang cannot be controlled,
it may be desirable to weaken its solidarity so that
the salvageable boys can be freed of its influence.

The solidarity of a group may be deliberately
weakened by a number of strategies: create dissension in the group over issues or status positions,
lessen the satisfactions it can offer, physically remove through imprisonment or foster-home placement
key members of the group, offer greater opportunities
elsewhere, reduce the prestige of the group, or deliberately lessen the trust gang members have of one
another. The latter strategy is mentioned by Ralph
Salerno (1969), a well-known authority in the field
of organized crime, in dealing with the syndicate.
He proposes starting rumors that this person or that
has already turned informer; publicizing syndicate
robberies as resulting in monetary losses greater
than those actually suffered, so the thieves will
think some of their members withheld part of the proceeds; and by substituting imitation for real gems
which the authorities already know are about to be
stolen, so that the thieves will fight over who got
the real gems.

4-2   THE NORMATIVE ASPECT OF REFERENCE GROUPS

We have just discussed the changing of behavior
by altering a person's choice of reference group. We
turn now to the problem of changing his behavior by
changing the normative system of the reference groups

with which he is presently identified. This is
achieved in a variety of ways: (1) sell the desired
norms and values directly to the target group; (2)
mediate between conventional norms and those of the
group; (3) show discrepancies within the group's normative system; (4) manipulate situations so as to (a)
increase communication flow from desired referents
and (b) make the normative system of the desired
group relevant; (5) secure commitment of the group to
change behavior in the direction desired; and (7)
provide rewards for desired change.

Sell Norms and Values to the Group

       Inasmuch as each group screens the information
flow from outside in terms of its own value system, a
problem of communication is to secure a credible and
trustworthy informant through whom law-abiding norms
and values can flow to the delinquent group with some
hope of favorable consideration. The Chicago Area
Project achieves this by the use of indigenous (local)
talent to organize and manage neighborhood settlement
and recreational activities. The local person has
the advantage of being familiar with the people of
the neighborhood, aware of its norms and values. He
speaks their language like the street-gang worker is
supposed to be able to do:

          "An important element in the worker's com-
     munication of norms and values to gang young-
     sters is his use of language, verbal and non-
     verbal, within a frame of reference which they
     can understand. He does not use perjorative
     or street language for the sake of random
     shock or to demonstrate he is 'one of the
     boys.' Change in the group will not occur,
     however, if the advice of the worker is given
     within a subcultural frame of reference which
     is foreign to them" (Spergel, 1966, p. 85).

The indigenous workers are accepted by those of the
neighborhood as sincere and trustworthy because they
are insiders and because they understand the local

situation. When recreational activities are run by such people the juveniles have a greater inclination to participate, since these activities are run by persons who to some degree are already role models of the youths, but who nonetheless support law-abiding behavior. In other words, the forces in the natural social world of the delinquent are utilized in the reformative process. The Boston Delinquency Project of Walter B. Miller (1959) also endeavored to utilize community support for the delinquency prevention program. Through activities in these two projects the adults and youths were able to gain recognition and to break down intraneighborhood tensions. Gangs became teams and engated in peaceful competition rather than conflict to determine their status.

Somewhat the same approach is suggested in rehabilitation of prisoners. Ideally, one would first sell a program to the most prestigeful inmates, the "right guys," perhaps by offering them some share in the planning, and then utilize their influence to get the program and its goals accepted by the rest of the prison population.

Mediate Between Conventional and Gang Norms

Sometimes compromises need to be made between two systems that are in conflict. The street-gang worker is in a favorable position to serve as a channel of communication between the conventional world and the delinquent group because he has the trust and confidence of each. Spergel (1966, p. 89) describes a worker in this role:

> "The worker encountered four members of the Silver Hawks who had just been ejected from the Community Center. The youngsters were angry and resentful. They asked the worker to plead with the agency director on their behalf. They said that they had done no wrong. The worker, however, was aware of what had occurred, and said the group members themselves were responsible for the disturbance

and, therefore, were thrown out. If they were
so interested in staying in the Center they
should have controlled their behavior. The
worker said finally that he was sorry about
what had happened and he could understand
their desire to get back, but he could not
really help them get back that night anyway.
He told them he would speak to the director of
the agency the following day. The boys seemed
to understand; at least they accepted the
worker's comments, and the worker escorted
them back to their part of the neighborhood."

Here the worker is seen as someone who is supportive,
and who cares, but who recognizes at the same time
the legitimacy of the rules of the Community Center.
We are not told how the worker ironed out the problem
the next day, but we may assume that some change was
made in the value system of the Silver Hawks and in
the comprehension of the boys' value system by the
Community Center director.

Show Discrepancies in the Group's Normative System

It is expected that one can change the attitudes
and behavior of law-violators through the creation of
cognitive dissonance by confronting them with the
discrepancy between their (a) norms and values, (b)
norms and their behavior, (c) values and behavior,
and (d) norms, values, and behavior as against that
of others with whom they identify. This might be
achieved by one or more of the following:

1. Probe to find their inconsistencies, and then
   confront them with the incongruities, especially those between their own norms and behavior on the one hand, and those of their
   avowed reference group on the other hand.
   This confrontation should be done by persons
   whose opinions cannot be shrugged off. It is
   for this reason that guided group interaction
   (Weeks, 1958) has been effective. In it the
   individual is interrogated by his own peers

under the guidance of a discussion leader.
The offender, who is explaining his own behavior, finds that his own peers recognize
that his rationalizations and defenses are
weak. He is forced to be honest (consistent)
with himself.

2. Find the identity that the offender is trying
   to establish, and then show that it is not
   consistent with his norms or his behavior.
   In this connection, the street-gang worker is
   advised by Spergel (1966, p. 85):

   "... The gang's own values may be
   used to raise questions about, and to
   advise against, certain unacceptable
   behavior. For example, gang youngsters want to be 'sharp' or 'cool' and
   'right." The worker may indicate to
   them ways of achieving these values by
   normative criteria which are conventionally acceptable. These new interpretations, norms, or redefinitions of
   behavior acceptable both to the group
   and the larger community may simply
   not have been thought of before. Prestige and status can sometimes be signi-
   fied in the same terms by the delinquent group and society. One worker
   reports his effort to change a group
   drinking pattern through the use of
   understandable language and a commonly
   accepted status symbol:

   "'I arrived at the street corner at
   9 p.m. ... Harry (18), Larry (19), Allen (18), and Frank (17) were there.
   We became engaged in a bull session
   about drinking. The boys were boasting
   about their experience with heavy drinking and drunkenness. I attempted to
   point out how ridiculous and even dangerous it was to become drunk. I explained how too much alcohol makes you
   lose your 'cool' and look and sound

> bad, etc. We talked about the differ-
> ence between drinking cheap wine from
> a bottle in an alley and sitting down
> and enjoying a highball like the 'man
> of distinction.'"

3. Find the goals he is seeking, and then show
   the goals are inconsistent with his behavior
   or the norms he is following.

4. Create a confrontation between the norms of
   two reference groups that he has compartmen-
   talized, by introducing both groups into one
   situation. As an example, his gang could be
   invited to visit his home or go along on a
   church picnic.

5. Show the discrepancy between the principles
   he espouses and his loyalty to an undesirable
   individual by exposing the motives and/or the
   behavior of the false model.

6. Convince him that others in his group have
   already changed their attitudes and behavior.
   He will then be forced to change either his
   reference group identification or the norms
   to which he now subscribes (Newcomb et al.,
   1965, p. 110). Even if he changes his reference group, there is some gain, for his norms
   will have less support than they did formerly.

Manipulate Situations

Situations may be manipulated to increase communication flow from desirable referents or to make a
particular normative orientation more pertinent.
These will be considered separately.

Increase the communication flow. The object
here is to increase communication flow between the
target group and desirable referents, while restricting the communication flow between the target group
and undesirable referents. In the prison community

this means increasing the interaction between guards
and inmates, and between inmates and their families,
while at the same time reducing the inmate-to-inmate
interaction (Glaser, 1964, p. 151 and 123). In the
free community there is less control over situations
than in prison, but social contacts of delinquents
with nondelinquent persons may be achieved by arranging for counselors to spend more time with boys in
need of guidance, Big Brothers to adopt needy boys,
street-club workers (and others) to aid boys in giving dances. Even compulsory attendance at school
assists in this objective. The probation and parole
rules which require persons under supervision not to
associate with others who have known criminal records
also have an influence (when observed) upon communication flow from undesirable quarters.

Increase the pertinence of the normative system.
This can be achieved by arranging for delinquent
groups to use the facilities of institutions which
are clearly identified with the conventional moral
order, e.g., churches, YMCA, Veterans Organizations,
Service Clubs, Settlement Houses, Police Athletic
Leagues, etc. These will call to mind the normative
system of the sponsoring agency, and influence the
behavior of the group.

Secure Commitments from Individuals

It is desirable to have a person who wants to
change his behavior to make a public commitment to
that effect, so that he will experience more cognitive dissonance if he begins to weaken his stand.
The signing of parole papers by an inmate being released is not a completely voluntary act, since it is
required for release on parole, but it does imply a
commitment by the signer to abide by the rules. A
bona fide commitment is considered essential on the
part of a patient who is undergoing psychotherapy, it
being essential that the patient be an active partic-
ipant in the treatment process (Jerome Frank, 1959).
It is here argued that social treatment as well as individual treatment requires commitment to be effective.

In a study of the treatment process used in Synanon in dealing with drug addicts, Volkman and Cressey (1963) reported that no person is admitted to treatment without making a firm commitment to stop using drugs once and for all. To prove he is committed, the addict may have to cut his hair, surrender all his money, or beg for a chance. Members of Alcoholics Anonymous must also make a public admission of being an alcoholic and in need of help. This surrender to the treatment group (former addicts or alcoholics) is an admission that one is weak, needs help of others to get rid of a terrible habit, and an acceptance of the norms by which the treatment group can function effectively.

Commitment to a treatment process should be active rather than passive. It is most effective when the individual accepts the responsibility to help others who have the same problem that he does. Donald Cressey (1955), in an article on changing criminals, describes the process of "retroflexive reformation" as follows:

> "The most effective mechanism for exerting group pressure on members will be found in groups so organized that criminals are induced to join with noncriminals for the purpose of changing other criminals. A group in which criminal A joins with some noncriminals to change criminal B is probably most effective in changing criminal A, not B; in order to change criminal B, criminal A must necessarily share the values of the anti-criminal group."

Secure Commitment from The Group

The group which is committed to reforming the individual will be more successful than one which considers reformation only as a by-product of some other activity. This means that the group norms are clearly committed to conventional values, norms, and morals. As an illustration, take the Synanon group

described by Volkman and Cressey (1963). Since the
group is committed to curing drug addicts, it takes a
strong antidrug stand. There is a strong taboo
against what is called "street-talk." A person is
reprimanded for talking about how it feels to take a
fix, who one's connection was, and the crimes he has
committed. He is not supposed to refer to conventional people as "squares." And whenever one member
of Synanon sees or hears about another violating any
of these norms, or engaging in any illegal behavior,
he must inform on him so that the others can have him
on the carpet for it. The same kind of norms could
develop in a half-way house or other organization
whose stated purpose is to help reintegrate the offender into society.

Reward Those Who Have Reformed

And lastly, within the group which is committed
to reforming men the social structure should be so
arranged that those making the most progress are accorded the highest status. This was found not only
in the Synanon group studied by Volkman and Cressey
(1963), but also in the Provo Experiment reported by
Empey and Rabow (1961). Society at large must also
provide acceptance and rewards for those who have
made the grade. Otherwise all talk about the need
for offenders to be reformed is hypocrisy, and the
strongest motive for the offender to reform is lost.
There are some indications that our society is moving
in this direction in becoming more humanitarian and
developing a social concern for the underprivileged,
but rapid progress is not anticipated in the immediate future.

REFERENCES

1. Aichhorn, August: *Wayward Youth* (New York: Viking Press, 1935).

2. Alexander, C. Norman, Jr., "Consensus and Mutual Attraction in Natural Cliques," *American Journal of Sociology*, 69 (January, 1964), 395-403.

3. Atkinson, John W. and Reitman, Walter R., "Performance as a Function of Motive Strength and Expectancy of Goal Attainment," Chapter 19 in *Motives in Fantasy, Action, and Society*, edited by John W. Atkinson (New York: D. Van Nostrand Company, Inc., 1958).

4. Back, K. W., "Influence through Communication," *Journal of Abnormal and Social Psychology*, 46 (1951), 9-24.

5. Backman, Carl W.; Secord, Paul F.; and Pierce, Jerry R., "Resistance to Change in the Self-Concept as a Function of Consensus among Significant Others," *Sociometry*, 26 (1963), 102-111, reprinted in Scott G. McNall: *The Sociological Perspective* (Boston: Little, Brown and Company, 1968), 165-74.

6. Bandura, Albert; Ross, Dorothy; and Ross, Sheila A., "A Comparative Test of the Status Envy, Social Power, and Secondary Reinforcement Theories of Identification Learning," *Journal of Abnormal and Social Psychology*, 67 (December, 1963), 527-537.

7. Bandura, Albert and Walters, R. H.: *Social Factors in Personality Development* (New York: Holt, Rinehart, and Winston, 1963).

8. Becker, Howard S.: *Outsiders: Studies in the Sociology of Deviance* (Glencoe, Illinois: The Free Press, 1963).

9. Berelson, Bernard and Steiner, Gary A.: *Human Behavior* (New York: Harcourt, Brace & World, Inc., 1964).

10. Blau, Peter M.: *Exchange and Power in Social
     Life* (New York: John Wiley and Sons, Inc.,
     1964).

11. Bram, Joseph: *Language and Society* (New York:
     Doubleday and Company, 1935).

12. Brehm, Jack W. and Cohen, Arthur R.: *Explora-
     tions in Cognitive Dissonance* (New York: John
     Wiley and Sons, Inc., 1962).

13. Briar, Scott and Piliavin, Irving, "Delinquency,
     Situational Inducements, and Commitment to Con-
     formity," *Social Problems*, 13 (Summer, 1965),
     35-45.

14. Brittain, Clay V., "Adolescent Choices and
     Parent-Peer Cross Pressures," *American Sociolog-
     ical Review*, 28 (June, 1963), 385-91.

15. Burgess, Robert L. and Akers, Ronald L., "A Dif-
     ferential Association-Reinforcement Theory of
     Criminal Behavior," *Social Problems*, 14 (Fall,
     1966), 128-47.

16. Cartwright, Dorwin, "Achieving Change in People:
     Applications of Group Dynamics Theory," *Human
     Relations*, 4 (1951), p. 388.

17. Clausen, John A., "Drug Addication," in Merton,
     Robert K. and Nisbet, Robert A.: *Contemporary
     Social Problems* (New York: Harcourt, Brace, and
     World, Inc., 1961), 181-221.

18. Clemmer, Donald: *The Prison Community* (Boston:
     The Christopher Publishing House, 1940).

19. Clinard, Marshall, "Criminological Research,"
     Chapter 23 in Merton, Robert K.: Broom, Leonard;
     and Cottress, Leonard S., Jr. (eds.): *Sociology
     Today: Problems and Prospects* (New York: Basic
     Books, Inc., 1959), 509-536.

20. Clinard, Marshall and Quinney, Richard: *Crimi-
     nal Behavior Systems: A Typology* (New York:
     Holt, Rinehart, and Winston, Inc., 1967).

21. Cloward, Richard A., and Ohlin, Lloyd, E.: *De-
     linquency and Opportunity* (Glencoe, Illinois:
     The Free Press, 1960).

22. Cohen, Albert K.: *Delinquent Boys* (Glencoe, Illinois: The Free Press, 1955).

23. Cohen, Albert K., "The Study of Social Disorganization and Deviant Behavior," in Merton, Robert K. et al. (eds.): *Sociology Today: Problems and Prospects* (New York: Basic Books, Inc., 1959), 461-84.

24. Cohen, Albert K. and Short, James F., "Juvenile Delinquency," in Merton, Robert K. and Nisbet, Robert A. (eds.): *Contemporary Social Problems* (New York: Harcourt, Brace, and World, Inc., 1961), 98-103.

25. Cohen, Albert K. and Hodges, Harold M., Jr., "Characteristics of the Lower Blue-Collar Class," *Social Problems*, 10 (Spring, 1963), 303-334.

26. Crawford, Paul; Malamud, Daniel I.; and Dumpson, James R., "Developing Relations with Teenage Gangs," in Johnston, Norman et al.: *The Sociology of Punishment and Correction*, Second Edition (New York: John Wiley and Sons, Inc., 1970), 627-634; reprinted with adaptations from *Working with Teenage Gangs* (New York: Welfare Council of New York City, 1950), 21-32, 34-35, 37-38.

27. Cressey, Donald R.: *Other People's Money* (Glencoe, Illinois: The Free Press, 1953).

28. Cressey, Donald R., "Changing Criminals: The Application of the Differential Association Theory," *American Journal of Sociology*, 61 (September, 1955), 116-20.

29. Cressey, Donald R., "The Theory of Differential Association: An Introduction," *Social Problems*, 8 (Summer, 1960), 2-5.

30. Cressey, Donald R., "The Language of Set Theory and Differential Association Theory," *The Journal of Research in Crime and Delinquency*, 3 (January, 1966), 22-26.

31. DeFleur, Melvin L. and Quinney, Richard, "A Reformulation of Sutherland's Differential Association Theory and a Strategy for Empirical Veri-

fication," *The Journal of Research in Crime and Delinquency*, 3 (January, 1966), 1-22.

32. Deutsch, Morton and Collins, Mary E.: *Interracial Housing and Psychological Revaluation of a Social Experiment* (Minneapolis: University of Minnesota Press, 1951).

33. Dornbusch, Sanford, "The Military Academy as an Assimilating Institution," *Social Forces*, 33 (May, 1955), 316-321.

34. Eisenstadt, S. M., "Reference Group Behavior and Social Integration: An Exploratory Study," *American Sociological Review*, 19 (April, 1954), 175-185.

35. Emerson, Richard, "Deviance and Rejection: An Experimental Replication," *American Sociological Review*, 19 (December, 1954), 688-693.

36. Empey, Lamar and Rabow, Jerome, "The Provo Experiment in Delinquency Prevention," *American Sociological Review*, 26 (October, 1961), 679-696.

37. Empey, Lamar, "Delinquency Theory and Recent Research," *Journal of Research in Crime and Delinquency*, 4 (January, 1967), 28-42.

38. Festinger, Leon; Schachter, Stanley; and Back, K. W.: *Social Pressures in Informal Groups: A Study of a Housing Community* (New York: Harper and Brothers, 1950).

39. Festinger, Leon, "A Theory of Social Comparison Processes," *Human Relations*, 7 (1954), 117-140.

40. Festinger, Leon: *A Theory of Cognitive Dissonance* (Evanston, Illinois: Harper, Row, and Peterson, Inc., 1957).

41. Frank, Jerome, "The Dynamics of the Psychotherapeutic Relationship," *Psychiatry*, 22 (February, 1959), 17-34; reprinted in Scheff, Thomas J. (ed.): *Mental Illness and Social Process* (New York: Harper, Row, and Co., 1967), 168-206.

42. Glaser, Daniel, "Criminality Theories and Behavior Images," *American Journal of Sociology*, 61 (March, 1956), 433-444.

43.   Glaser, Daniel, "Differential Association and Criminological Prediction," *Social Problems*, 8 (Summer, 1960), 6-13.

44.   Glaser, Daniel: *The Effectiveness of a Prison and Parole System* (New York: The Bobbs-Merrill Company, Inc., 1964).

45.   Glueck, Sheldon and Glueck, Eleanor: *Unravelling Juvenile Delinquency* (New York: Commonwealth Fund, 1950).

46.   Gouldner, Alvin and Gouldner, Helen P.: *Modern Sociology* (New York: Harcourt, Brace and World, Inc., 1963).

47.   Greenwald, Harold G.: *The Call Girl* (New York: Ballantine Books, 1958).

48.   Hall, Peter M., "Identification with Delinquent Subculture and Level of Self-Evaluation," *Sociometry*, 29 (June, 1966), 146-158; reprinted in Lefton, Mark et al. (eds.): *Approaches to Deviance* (New York: Appleton-Century-Crofts, 1968), 266-278.

49.   Hartley, Ruth E., "Norm Compatibility, Norm Preferences, and the Acceptance of New Reference Groups," *Journal of Social Psychology*, 52 (1960), 87-95.

50.   Hartshorne, H. and May, M. A.: *Studies in Deceit*. Book I. (New York: The Macmillan Co., 1928).

51.   Haskell, Martin R., "Toward a Reference Group Theory of Juvenile Delinquency," *Social Problems*, 8 (Winter, 1960), 220-230.

52.   Havighurst, R. J. et al.: *Growing up in River City* (New York: John Wiley and Sons, Inc., 1962).

53.   Healy, William and Bronner, Augusta F.: *New Light on Delinquency and Its Treatment* (New Haven: Yale University Press, 1936).

54.   Homans, George C.: *The Human Group* (New York: Harcourt, Brace and World, Inc., 1950).

55. Homans, George C.: *Sentiments and Activities* (Glencoe, Illinois: The Free Press, 1962), 91-102.

56. Hyman, Herbert, "The Psychology of Status," *Archives of Psychology*, 269 (June, 1942), p. 15.

57. Inkeles, Alex, "Society, Social Structure, and Child Socialization," in John Clausen (ed): *Socialization and Society* (Boston: Little, Brown, and Co., 1968), pp. 73-129.

58. Irwin, John: *The Felon* (Englewood Cliffs, N. J.: Prentice-Hall, Inc., 1970).

59. Jansyn, Leon R., Jr., "Solidarity and Delinquency in a Street Corner Group," *American Sociological Review*, 31 (October, 1966), pp. 600-614.

60. Kaplan, Norman: *Reference Group Theory and Voting Behavior*, Columbia University Doctoral Dissertation, unpublished, 1955.

61. Kelley, Harold H. and Volkart, Edmund H., "The Resistance to Change of Group Anchored Attitudes," *American Sociological Review*, 17 (April, 1952), 453-65.

62. Kelman, Herbert C., "Processes of Opinion Change," *Public Opinion Quarterly*, 25 (1961), 55-77.

63. Kemper, Theodore, "Reference Groups, Socialization, and Achievement," *American Sociological Review*, 33 (February, 1968), 31-45.

64. Klapp, Orrin E.: *Heroes, Villains, and Fools* (Englewood Cliffs, N. J.: Prentice Hall, Inc., a Spectrum Book, S-31, 1962).

65. Kobrin, Solomon, "The Chicago Area Project--a 25 Year Assessment," *The Annals of the American Academy of Political and Social Science*, 322 (March, 1959), 20-29.

66. Kobrin, Solomon; Puntil, Joseph; and Pelusco, Emil, "Criteria of Status Among Street Groups," *Journal of Research in Crime and Delinquency*, 4 (January, 1967), 98-118.

67. Kohlberg, Lawrence: *Stages in the Development of Moral Thought and Action* (New York: Holt, Rinehart, and Winston, 1969). Also, see Kohlbert's "Stage and Sequence: The Cognitive Development Approach to Socialization," pp. 347-380 in David G. Goslin (ed.): *Handbook of Socialization Theory and Research* (Chicago: Rand McNalley, 1969).

68. Kvaraceus, William C. and Miller, Walter B.: *Delinquent Behavior: Culture and the Individual* (Washington, D. C.: National Education Association of the United States, 1959).

69. Landesco, John, "Organized Crime in Chicago, *The Illinois Crime Survey, Part III* (Chicago: Illinois Association for Criminal Justice, 1929).

70. Laulicht, Jerome, "Role Conflict, the Pattern Variability Theory, and Scalogram Analysis," *Social Forces*, 33 (March, 1955), p. 250.

71. Lemert, Edwin M., "An Isolation and Closure Theory of Naive Check Forgery," *Journal of Criminal Law, Criminology, and Police Science*, 44 (September-October, 1953), 296-307.

72. Lemert, Edwin M.: *Human Deviance, Social Problems and Social Control* (Englewood Cliffs, N. J.: Prentice-Hall, Inc., 1967), Chapter 9, "Role Enactment, Self, and Identity in the Systematic Check Forger," 119-134.

73. Liska, Allen E., "Interpreting the Causal Structure of the Differential Association Theory," *Social Problems*, 16 (Spring, 1969), 485-492.

74. Lofland, John: *Deviance and Identity* (Englewood Cliffs, N. J.: Prentice-Hall, Inc., 1969).

75. McClosky, Herbert and Dahlgren, Harold W., "Primary Group Influences on Party Loyalty," in Simpson, Richard L. and Simpson, Ida Harper (eds.): *Social Organization and Behavior* (New York: John Wiley and Sons, Inc., 1964), 209-226.

76. McHugh, Peter, "Social Disintegration as a Requisite to Resocialization," *Social Forces*, XLIV (March, 1966), 355-363.

77. Maccoby, Eleanor E., "Moral Values and Behavior in Childhood," in John A. Clausen (ed.): *Socialization and Society* (Boston: Little, Brown and Co., 1968), 227-269.

78. Matthews, Victor, "Differential Identification: An Empirical Note," *Social Problems*, 15 (Winter, 1968), 376-383.

79. Matza, David: *Delinquency and Drift* (New York: John Wiley and Sons, Inc., 1964).

80. Merton, Robert K.: *Social Theory and Social Structure* (Glencoe, Illinois: The Free Press, 1957), 225-259.

81. Miller, Walter B., "Preventive Work with Street Corner Groups: Boston Delinquency Project," *The Annals of the American Academy of Political and Social Science*, 322 (March, 1959), 97-106.

82. Mizruchi, Ephraim: *Success and Opportunity: A Study of Anomie* (Glencoe, Illinois: The Free Press, 1964).

83. Newcomb, Theodore M.: *Social Psychology* (New York: The Dryden Press, Inc., 1950).

84. Newcomb, Theodore M., "The Prediction of Interpersonal Attraction," *American Psychologist*, 60 (1956), 575-586.

85. Newcomb, Theodore M., "The Study of Consensus," in Merton, Robert K. et al. (eds.): *Sociology Today: Problems and Prospects* (New York: Basic Books, Inc., 1959), 277-292.

86. Newcomb, Theodore M.: *The Acquaintance Process* (New York: Holt, Rinehart, and Winston, Inc., 1961).

87. Newcomb, Theodore M.; Turner, Ralph H.; and Converse, Philip E.: *Social Psychology* (New York: Holt, Rinehart, and Winston, Inc., 1965).

88. Parsons, Talcott and Shils, Edward A. (eds.): *Toward a General Theory of Social Action* (New York: Harper Torchbooks, TB 1083, 1951).

89. Piaget, J.: *The Moral Judgment of the Child* (Glencoe, Illinois: The Free Press, 1948). Translation of book originally published in 1932.

90. Plant, James S.: *Personality and the Cultural Pattern* (New York: Commonwealth Fund, 1937).

91. Reckless, Walter C.; Dinitz, Simon; and Murray, Ellen, "Self-Concept as an Insulator Against Delinquency," *American Sociological Review*, 21 (December, 1956), 744-746.

92. Redl, Fritz and Wineman, David: *Children Who Hate* (Glencoe, Illinois: The Free Press, 1951).

93. Rosenfeld, Eva, "A Research-Based Proposal for a Community Program of Delinquency Prevention," *The Annals of the American Academy of Political and Social Science*, 322 (March, 1959), 136-145.

94. Salerno, Ralph: *The Crime Confideration* (Garden City, N. Y.: Doubleday, 1969).

95. Schachter, Stanley, "Deviation, Rejection and Communication," *Journal of Abnormal and Social Psychology*, 47 (1951), 190-207.

96. Secord, Paul F. and Backman, Carl W.: *Social Psychology* (New York: McGraw-Hill Book Co., 1964).

97. Seeman, Marvin, "Role Conflict and Ambivalence in Leadership," *American Sociological Review*, 18 (August, 1953), 373-380.

98. Shaw, Clifford R.: *The Jack-Roller: A Delinquent Boy's Own Story* (Chicago: University of Chicago Press, 1930).

99. Shaw, Clifford R., "Juvenile Delinquency: A Group Tradition," *Child Welfare Pamphlets*, No. 24, Bulletin of the State University of Iowa, Iowa City, 1933; reprinted in Short, James F. (ed.): *Gang Delinquency and Delinquent Subcultures* (New York: Harper, Row, and Co., 1968), 82-92.

100. Shaw, Clifford R.: *Brothers in Crime* (Chicago: The University of Chicago Press, 1938).

101. Sherif, Muzafer and Cantril, Handley: *The Psy-chology of Ego-Involvements* (New York: Wiley and Sons, Inc., 1947).

102. Sherif, Muzafer, "Reference Groups in Human Re-lations," in Sherif, Muzafer and Wilson, M. O.: *Group Relations at the Crossroads* (New York: Harper and Brothers, 1953), 203-231.

103. Sherif, Muzafer and Sherif, Carolyn: *Reference Groups* (New York: Harper and Row, Publishers, 1964).

104. Sherif, Muzafer and Sherif, Carolyn: *Problems of Youth* (Chicago: Aldine Publishing Co., 1965).

105. Shibutani, Tamotsu, "Reference Groups as Per-spectives," *American Journal of Sociology*, 60 (May, 1955), 562-569.

106. Shibutani, Tamotsu: *Society and Personality* (Englewood Cliffs, N. J.: Prentice-Hall, Inc., 1961).

107. Short, James F., Jr., "Differential Association as a Hypothesis: Problems of Empirical Test-ing," *Social Problems*, 8 (Summer, 1960), 14-24.

108. Short, James F., Jr. and Strodtbeck, Frederick L.: *Group Process and Gang Delinquency* (Chica-go: The University of Chicago Press, 1965).

109. Slavson, S. R.: *Re-educating the Delinquent Through Group and Community Participation* (New York: Harper and Brothers, 1954).

110. Spergel, Irving: *Racketville, Slumtown, Haul-burg* (Chicago: The University of Chicago Press, 1964).

111. Spergel, Irving: *Street Gang Work: Theory and Practice* (Reading, Mass.: Addison-Wesley Pub-lishing Company, Inc., 1966).

112. Staats, Arthur: *An Integrated-Functional Learn-ing Approach to Complex Human Behavior*, Techni-cal Report 28, Contract ONR and Arizona State University, 1965.

113. Stephenson, Richard M. and Scarpitti, Frank R.,
      "Argot in a Therapeutic Milieu," *Social Prob-
      lems*, 15 (Winter, 1968), 384-395.

114. Stouffer, Samuel A., "An Analysis of Conflict-
      ing Social Norms," *American Sociological Review*,
      14 (December, 1949), 707-717.

115. Stouffer, Samuel A. and Toby, Jackson, "Role
      Conflict and Personality," in Parsons, Talcott
      and Shils, Edward (eds.): *Toward a General
      Theory of Social Action* (New York: Harper
      Torchbooks, TB 1083, 1962), 481-493.

116. Sullivan, Harry Stack: *The Interpersonal The-
      ory of Psychiatry* (New York: W. W. Norton and
      Company, 1953), 223-225.

117. Sumner, William Graham: *Folkways* (New York:
      Ginn & Co., 1906).

118. Sutherland, Edwin H., "White-Collar Criminali-
      ty," *American Sociological Review*, 5 (February,
      1940), 10-11.

119. Sutherland, Edwin H., "Development of a Theory,"
      address given to the Ohio Valley Sociological
      Society, April, 1942, published in Cohen, Al-
      bert et al.: *The Sutherland Papers* (Blooming-
      ton: Indiana University Press, 1956).

120. Sutherland, Edwin H.: *Principles of Criminol-
      ogy*, Fourth Edition (Chicago: J. B. Lippincott
      Co., 1947).

121. Suttles, Gerald D.: *The Social Order of the
      Slum* (Chicago: The University of Chicago Press,
      1968).

122. Sykes, Gresham and Matza, David, "Techniques of
      Neutralization, A Theory of Delinquency," *Amer-
      ican Sociological Review*, 22 (December, 1957),
      664-670.

123. Tefferteller, Ruth S., "Delinquency Prevention
      Through Revitalizating Parent-Child Relations,"
      *The Annals of the American Academy of Political
      and Social Science*, 322 (March, 1959), 67-78.

124. Thibaut, John W. and Kelley, Harold: *The So-cial Psychology of Groups* (New York: John Wiley and Sons, Inc., 1961).

125. Thomas, W. I.: *The Unadjusted Girl* (Boston: Little, Brown, and Co., 1923).

126. Thrasher, Frederick M.: *The Gang* (Chicago: The University of Chicago Press, 1926).

127. Turner, Ralph H., "Value-Conflict in Social Disorganization," *Sociology and Social Research*, 38 (1954), 301-308.

128. Turner, Ralph H., "Reference Groups and Future-Oriented Men," *Social Forces*, 34 (1955), 131.

129. Turner, Ralph H., "Role-Taking, Role Standpoint, and Reference Group Behavior," *American Journal of Sociology*, 61 (January, 1956), 316-328.

130. Turner, Ralph H.: *The Social Context of Ambition* (San Francisco: The Chandler Publishing Co., 1964).

131. Turner, Ralph H., "Upward Mobility and Class Values," *Social Problems*, 11 (Spring, 1964), 359-371.

132. Volkman, Rita and Cressey, Donald R., "Differential Association and the Rehabilitation of Drug Addicts," *American Journal of Sociology*, 69 (September, 1963), 129-142.

133. Wade, Andrew L., "Social Processes in the Act of Juvenile Vandalism," in Clinard, Marshall and Quinney, Richard (eds.): *Criminal Behavior Systems: A Typology* (New York: Holt, Rinehart, and Winston, Inc., 1967), 94-109.

134. Weeks, H. Ashley: *Youthful Offenders at High-fields* (Ann Arbor: The University of Michigan Press, 1958).

135. Whyte, William F.: *Street Corner Society*, Second Edition (Chicago: The University of Chicago Press, 1958).

136. Whyte, William H, Jr.: *The Organization Man* (New York: Simon and Schuster, 1956).

137. Weinberg, S. Kirsen, "Personality and Method in the Differential Association Theory," *Journal of Research in Crime and Delinquency*, 3 (July, 1966), 165-172.

138. Wirth, Louis, "Culture Conflict and Misconduct," *Social Forces*, 9 (June, 1931), 484-492.

139. Wolfgang, Marvin: *Patterns in Criminal Homicide* (Philadelphia: University of Pennsylvania Press, 1958).

140. Yablonsky, Lewis, "The Delinquent Gang as a Near Group," *Social Problems*, 7 (Fall, 1959), 108-117.

141. Vander Zanden, James W.: *Sociology: A Systematic Approach* (New York: The Ronald Press, 1965).

SUBJECT INDEX

INDEX OF NAMES